The
Divine
Heart

ALSO BY *Colette Lafia*

Comfort and Joy: Simple Ways to Care for Ourselves and Others

*Seeking Surrender: How My Friendship with a Trappist Monk
Taught Me to Trust and Embrace Life*

The Divine Heart

SEVEN WAYS TO LIVE IN GOD'S LOVE

Colette Lafia

Monkfish Book Publishing Company
Rhinebeck, New York

Paperback ISBN 978-1-948626-37-8
eBook ISBN 978-1-948626-38-5

Cover design by Lisa Carta
Book design by Colin Rolfe

Library of Congress Cataloging-in-Publication Data

Names: Lafia, Colette, author.
Title: The divine heart : seven ways to live in God's love / Colette Lafia.

Description: Rhinebeck, New York : Monkfish Book Publishing Company, 2021.
 | Includes bibliographical references.
Identifiers: LCCN 2020050481 (print) | LCCN 2020050482 (ebook) | ISBN
 9781948626378 (paperback) | ISBN 9781948626385 (ebook)
Subjects: LCSH: Spiritual life--Catholic Church. | Spirituality--Catholic
 Church.
Classification: LCC BX2350.5 .L28 2021 (print) | LCC BX2350.5 (ebook) |
 DDC 248.4/82--dc23
LC record available at https://lccn.loc.gov/2020050481
LC ebook record available at https://lccn.loc.gov/2020050482

Monkfish Book Publishing Company
22 East Market Street, Suite 304
Rhinebeck, NY 12572
(845) 876-4861
monkfishpublishing.com

To All Those Who Have Mentored My Heart

CONTENTS

PERMISSIONS

PROLOGUE

Learning to love is our human mission, one we're all on together. Yet during the coronavirus pandemic, our frayed hearts have been dragged through uncertainty and loss along unmarked trails. We've been trudging through our days practicing social distancing, wearing masks, connecting with people virtually, and feeling disoriented a lot of the time. We've been living with a sadness that never seems to go away, accumulating like the dust and rain that stain our windows.

A month into the Covid-19 shutdown, my beloved father-in-law, Brian, passed away. He didn't have the coronavirus, but it indirectly played a role. He was unable to receive a "nonessential" hospital procedure and died of complications from his condition. Attending his online burial and family gatherings to honor him was heartbreaking. But it was also a gift. From the humorous, loving, and poignant stories shared about him, it was clear that those who knew him felt well-loved and accepted by him. In this river of loss, he had left a legacy of love—a powerful and resonant love we would not forget. I was reminded that love is what lingers— and shimmers—even in times of pain and grief.

Shortly after we started sheltering in place, I began rereading *New Seeds of Contemplation* by the Christian monk Thomas Merton, poring over his writings on solitude. I was drawn to his concept that *solitude is not separation*. Solitude's purpose, Merton said, is to help "you to love not only God but also people."

An image I have been holding during this time of solitude is that of a tree in a forest. Like an individual tree, I know I'm connected to a network of trees and that our root systems intersect and grow into one another's below the ground. Like trees, we live in cooperative, interdependent relationships, share nutrients, and are connected to the whole—the great forest of the world held together in Divine love.

How can sheltering in place and the deep suffering of lost jobs and lost lives also be embraced as a time of renewal? Perhaps there are ways we can welcome this pause from rushing around and consuming, from decades of restlessness and discontent. For besides the pain and loss, this has been a time for kids to ride bikes and for hummingbirds to feast on the renewed abundance of nectar.

Born of love is hope. Now, as we are called to integrate so much paradox and pain, we need guidance to heal, strengthen, and restore ourselves. *The Divine Heart* offers this guidance, outlining ways we can learn to grow and renew ourselves in Divine love. Each of us has a Divine heart, an identity we share. We not only align ourselves with love and connect to love, but we also recognize that we *are* love.

Consider *The Divine Heart* a guidebook to help you find your way around this new landscape that is filled with loss and hope yet at the same time offers new possibilities when you look with the eyes of the heart. As you open this book, listen to the longing in your heart and allow yourself to embark on a spiritual renewal, a journey into the Divine heart, into unity, connection, and belonging. God is in us and we are in God, and there is an unfolding intimacy between us—with the Divine, with one another, and with our mother, the earth. It is a complete and mutual indwelling.

Can we dare say that this time, with so many tears, is also a time of spiritual rebirth, a time to awaken to the fullness of love, to connect ourselves more fully to the love we all share and dwell in, individually and collectively? My answer is *yes,* we *can* use our suffering to connect ourselves more fully to love.

As I grieved the death of my father-in-law, and a month later the loss of my older brother, along with the news of so many other people dying and experiencing loss, I sat in my sadness reaching for love. Love can hold and heal and transform pain—but not an abstract love. We can learn to love beyond what we thought we were capable of. Our heart, living in the Divine heart, in the heart of the world, has a capacity that is boundless. It is the source of life itself and will help us find our way through this time of grief and uncertainty.

Once in the flow of Divine love, we realize this love has been here all along waiting for us. A retreat, a book, a conversation, a pandemic—anything can open our hearts to that love, and we can allow it to enter us. Anything can engender a spiritual renewal in our heart and be, for us, a source of hope and gratitude. I invite you to open to your own heart and to the hearts of others. In the depth and breadth of our sadness, we will find grace, love, and a way forward.

PART I

BEGINNINGS

AWAKENING TO THE FLOW OF GOD'S LOVE

On a warm Sunday afternoon a few years ago, following an extremely busy week, I relished the opportunity for unstructured time. At last, I could slow down and go to my art studio to take care of simple tasks like recycling papers, shelving books, and tidying up. My husband was outside tending our garden, trimming overgrown jasmine, pulling up the weeds that had popped up everywhere after the winter rains, and planting petunias in porcelain pots. As I settled into peace, making order in my studio, I enjoyed listening to the rustle of his activity.

I began placing pastels into a small basket and tightening the caps on the acrylic paints, when a flash of inspiration coursed through me. With my fingers tingling, I spontaneously pinned seven large sheets of paper on the wall and drew images and wrote the words that were pouring through me. After perhaps thirty minutes, I felt complete—my fingertips stained, my heart still racing. I looked at the papers and saw a series of abstract drawings with a single word scribbled in large charcoal letters on each piece: "Receptivity," "Delight," "Expansiveness," "Acceptance," "Vulnerability," "Mystery," and "Gratitude." Every drawing was covered with smudges, marks, thin lines, spirals, and circles intimating revelations yet to be discovered. I paused, looked again with soft-focused eyes and envisaged the common thread: the unfolding intimacy of my relationship with the Divine.

From that moment of grace, I began to write this book, and as I've continued exploring these qualities of love, I now see each one as an *invitation* to uncover the depth of love and awaken to our connection and union with the Divine, and with everyone and everything else.

"The Shape of God"

While working on this book, I enrolled in a two-year, spiritual-formation program in the Christian contemplative and mystical traditions at the Living School in New Mexico. During a symposium presented by Father Richard Rohr, a Franciscan priest and globally recognized ecumenical teacher, I was struck by his words, "If we don't get the shape of God right, everything wobbles."

By "shape of God," Father Richard was referring to the Holy Trinity. From what I understand, he sees the Father/Mother as *Fountain Fullness*, a flow of infinite love that fills all things; the Son/Word as *Incarnation*, the outpouring of love and the reality that spirit and matter are inseparable;

and the Holy Spirit as *Indwelling Love, Grace, and Energy*. When I asked him to explain further, he said simply, "Think of the Trinity as the dynamic flow of love."

Love is always present in all created things and always offering itself. God is, thus, a relationship, one in which we can participate in every moment. Divine love is utterly dynamic. Hearing Father Richard, I felt affirmed in the direction I was being guided.

In this book, I use the language of relationship to write about Divine love. I invite you to join me in bringing your relationship with Divine love into your connection with everyone and everything in your life. St. John of the Cross called Divine love "the template and model for all human love, and human love as the necessary school and preparation for any transcendent encounter."[1] We grow up hearing "God is love," but how do we cultivate this utmost important relationship?

Awakening to Love

> I desired you before the world began
> I desire you now
> As you desire me.
> And where the desires of two come together
> There love is perfected.
>
> — MECHTHILD OF MAGDEBURG[2]

---

[1] Quoted by Richard Rohr in *The Naked Now: Learning to See as the Mystics See* (New York: The Crossroad Publishing Company, 2009), 140.

[2] Jane Hirshfield, ed., *Women in Praise of the Sacred: 43 Centuries of Spiritual Poetry by Women* (New York: HarperCollins, 1995), 88.

Our lives are made up of raw, "in-between" moments, intimate and unfolding, those moments when God catches us unadorned. They happen of their own accord, carried on the wings of grace, when we're undressing, when we lie awake in bed in the early-morning silence, when a child reaches up to hold our hand. They take place when we help our elderly parent with grocery shopping, or when we're lost in the reverie of watching the ocean waves. They happen when we receive the Eucharist at Mass, or when we melt into a lover's kiss. These moments create markers in our hearts, moments of recognition when we're struck by something unexpected, and they leave us awakened and touched deeply.

When I was seven, God came to me in an instant. It was a hot, humid summer afternoon in Biscayne Bay, Florida, the air was thick with moisture, my skin covered with sweat. Wearing a red plaid polyester short set my mother had bought for me at Kmart, I was running through the grass in our backyard kicking a rubber ball into the air, catching it, kicking it, and catching it again. I loved being outdoors, alone, away from the noise of my brothers and sisters and from my alcoholic mother hiding in the bedroom.

Just then I heard a seagull's plaintive call and looked up, barely able to see the gull's white, flapping wings soaring by. Suddenly, I was overcome with a sense of *vastness*—as though I *was* that seagull flying freely in the infinitely blue sky—one moment heard, the next moment gone. And there I was, my little feet planted on the ground, guided by my soaring spirit. From that day on, I knew I was a part of something bigger. I began sensing the presence of God everywhere, in things large and small. God was in my rubber ball, my messy family, the crystal blue sky, the seagull, God was in *everything*. That day, touching the vastness of life, my heart grew.

When I was twenty-three, God surprised me again. I was living in San Francisco studying for a teaching credential. I didn't have a car, so I took public buses. On a September afternoon on my way to school, riding the local Mission District bus that seemed to be stopping at every corner, I got hotter and hotter to the point of exhaustion. The bus was overcrowded, and grocery bags lined the aisles; the air smelled of tortillas, sweat, and shampoo.

I was standing in the back, holding on to the overhead handle as the bus bumped over what seemed like every pothole. My heavy backpack resting at my feet, I looked down the aisle, packed with people and shopping bags, and suddenly my heart expanded into waves of love that were flowing in and out of me. Everyone and everything was absorbed within this singular vision, and I had the overwhelming sense of not being separate from anyone—of being connected to *all* in God's love. In the thick of the clatter, rumbling, and strong smells, my heart burst open.

The framework I'd confined myself within—the boundaries that had held me apart from others—dissolved. A gentle breeze swept through me and, it seemed, through the entire bus. I knew in the depths of my being that we're all expressions of Divine love, no one more and none less than another. I prayed this realization would stay with me and be consecrated.

God Is a Love Relationship

My experience of the Divine entering the ordinary moments of my life created in me an inner stirring. It felt active and alive, like a fluttering butterfly or a green plant stem pushing up from the dark soil. Something had awakened in me—a profound sense of Sacred presence and the awareness that I was not separate from the Divine. I felt a longing for an even deeper union with God, for a growing consciousness that I am living inside this Divine love, and this Divine love lives inside of me.

As the years went by and I moved through a series of jobs from nonprofit director to elementary school librarian, staying steady in a loving marriage that faced infertility, my urge for more intimacy with God continued to grow. I wanted to live out the commandment to "love the Lord your God with all your heart and with all your soul and with all your strength and with all your mind."[3] My burning question was how—how to nurture Divine intimacy.

Last winter, the answer came. I'd returned home from a long day of work, then grocery shopping, and finally a last-minute yoga class. I sat on the edge of my bed, drained

---

[3] Deuteronomy 6:5, Mark 12:30, Matthew 22:37, and Luke 10:27 (NRSV).

and ready for a warm bath, and I prayed, *Dear God, let me not forget that you are with me through all of this.*

As I slipped out of my clothes, my eyes landed on a single pink rose in a slender vase my husband had placed on the dresser. My gaze lingered, and I felt an invisible unfurling of something within me. In the stillness, my heart cracked open and God's boundless love flooded my being. I knew I was returning home to the place where the Divine has always been and would always be waiting for me, inside myself. Everything I need, I could see, is already in the beautiful bud of my heart. God's generous love is always there. We're born knowing this, and although we might forget, this is our spiritual heritage and our spiritual intuition.

At that moment, I heard these words clearly within me: *God is a love relationship.* Like the rose on my dresser opening to the light, my heart was opening to the Divine. This unfurling, like the petals of the rose, seeks and needs to open. That is its purpose and its destiny, and in that moment, it was both obvious *and* a revelation. We are, in every moment, living a Divine love relationship.

The Divine Unfurling

Over the next few days, I watched layer upon layer of rose petals slowly appear in the vase on my dresser, bringing the deep pink flower into inexpressible magnificence. As it opened, I felt as though I were glimpsing the Divine love relationship I was already living—tender, dynamic, and delightful. I felt God's love blooming within me, and I was flowering in it. I could sense the Divine intimacy I am always living, as is everyone else. In a moment of despair, getting ready to bathe before dinner, I found what I'd been longing for—the Divine home of my heart, the access point for God's intimate love. For me, the rose became a symbol of this unfolding. From bud to flower, our hearts open and reach out to the Divine. This intimate heart recognizes it's a dwelling place for the Divine and that it lives and grows within the heart of God.

In moments like seeing the seagull, riding the city bus, and sitting on the edge of my bed, exhausted, I discovered that my love relationship with the Divine is a living, searching, learning journey. This unfolding dynamic keeps growing and changing as I discover new ways to navigate the world. I now know that I am connected to a vast, expanding love that is within and around me. As intimacy with the Divine grows, so does a more intimate relationship with myself, with others, and with nature, art, and sacred ritual. Each is an encounter of the heart, with Divine love at its core.

And when I'm mindful of it all, I can see the cross-fertilization of the sacred with my ordinary daily life. My love relationship with the Divine brings me closer to the particulars of my own life, and at the same time, my intimacy in all my relationships brings me closer to God. Love for the Divine and love within are reciprocal, and I know I'm a full participant. As thirteenth-century philosopher and mystic

Meister Eckhart said, "The eye through which I see God is the eye through which God sees me; my eye and God's eye are one eye, one seeing, one knowing, one love."[4]

Each of our experiences of the Divine is uniquely personal, a truth we must honor and claim, and yet, at the core we share the same bond to Divine love. This is a love relationship not unlike those we long for with our spouses, parents, and friends—a connection that nourishes and holds our very souls. Every day we're called to live in and experience this unfolding intimacy with the Divine, and it makes my soul feel light, like lace on a veil. As I feel this lightness, I hold the Divine close, closer than my own breath. I find shelter with God—the Divine, Holy, Sweet One, Comforter, and Friend, the One Who Loves Me into Being in Every Moment.

---

[4] *The Complete Mystical Works of Meister Eckhart*, trans. Maurice C. Walsh (New York: The Crossroad Publishing Company, 2009), 298.

PART II

SEVEN WAYS
INVITING DIVINE LOVE INTO YOUR LIFE

"If you have never experienced human love, it will be very hard for you to access God as Love. If you have never let God love you, you will not know how to love humanly in the deepest way."

— RICHARD ROHR[1]

D uring the epiphany I experienced that Sunday afternoon with pencils, pastels, and charcoal, I discovered these seven ways of inviting in God's love. Underlying each is a question similar to one posed by James Finley, another core faculty member of the Living School: *"How do you give yourself over to that which is giving itself to you?"*[2]

---

[1] Rohr, *The Naked Now*, 140.
[2] Offered by James Finley during a retreat on St. Teresa of Avila, November 10-12, 2017.

THE FIRST INVITATION – RECEPTIVITY

When I was a child, my parents brought me to Mass every Sunday. When I turned seven, I was able to receive the Holy Communion. Each week, I eagerly awaited walking up the aisle to receive God's life into me. I would kneel in silence as the host dissolved slowly on my tongue, feeling union with the Divine, who was alive inside me. This kind of receptivity, grounded in what Finley calls "childlike sincerity," allows us to hear what cannot be known without Divine presence and to receive the love God continuously pours into us.

THE SECOND INVITATION – DELIGHT

When we enjoy the sensations of life, God is there. We feel Divine love when we run in the sand, laugh in the rain, or drink in the night air. "Here we go, God," I say as I get on my bicycle and head off to work. The trip takes me through Golden Gate Park, and as I ride along, the fog-filled air cooling my face, eucalyptus and cypress trees towering above me, I'm filled with wonder and freedom, in awe of the power of creation. The world is God's fingerprint and footprint, as St. Bonaventure, the thirteenth-century Franciscan, tells us.[3] Every day, we can allow ourselves to sense the landscapes of our heart and live fully in the world with Spirit as our guide.

---

[3] *Bonaventure*, ed. Ewert Cousins, Classics of Western Spirituality (Mahwah, NJ: Paulist Press, 1978), 77.

THE THIRD INVITATION – EXPANSIVENESS

Through expansiveness we open to the depths and breadth of our inner landscape, especially the realm of the heart where "with God all things are possible."[4] When we join our heart with God and allow it to keep opening and expanding, we can feel our own heart-center grow in resonance with the heart of God. The more deeply Divine love grows in us, the greater cosmic love expands. We learn to live in the world with all beings as a sacred and holy place. Leaning into grace, we trust that the love we encounter will keep opening.[5] As my mother told me when she was ninety, long after she'd gotten sober and found her own love within, *"To love God is to be open to letting God love you."*

THE FOURTH INVITATION – ACCEPTANCE

Can we allow ourselves to be accepted by God, by others, and ourselves without pretense or posturing? Can we be held completely by Divine love, just as we are? We're being kneaded and formed by God's loving hands. The more we're willing to meet all of ourselves, the more we can be touched by Divine love's tenderness. We pray for the grace to accept God's unconditional acceptance of us, God's compassion, loving kindness, and mercy. We hear the encouraging words, "There is no place I cannot reach," and are called to live in accord with the words of Trappist monk Thomas Merton: "The root of Christian love is not the will to love, but the

---

[4] Matthew 19:26 (NRSV).
[5] Christian Wiman, *My Bright Abyss: Meditation of a Modern Believer* (New York: Farrar, Straus and Giroux, 2013), 23.

faith that one is loved. That faith that one is loved by God although unworthy—or, rather, irrespective of one's worth!"[6]

THE FIFTH INVITATION – VULNERABILITY

To have a personal relationship with God, we must reveal to God, and thus ourselves, our most vulnerable, hidden places, filled with fear and uncertainty, as well as sweetness and longing. Allowing ourselves to be more and more seen takes courage and honesty. In spiritual direction, we say, "Come as you are. *All of you* is welcome." Hear God saying those words to you, and feel yourself held in Divine love, as you are, completely. This is necessary to be in a loving relationship with the Divine.

THE SIXTH INVITATION – MYSTERY

Inherent in all our love relationships—with the Divine, creation, one another, and ourselves—there exists wonder, magnitude, and the power of *mystery*. I met my husband on a winter's night at a café in Montréal. As our eyes met, we stepped into each other's hearts. Mystery is what we are and what life brings us. We are born touched by mystery, living in relationship with God's mysterious love, an embrace that envelops us wholly. Deep calls upon deep, as we become more present to this sacred love, guided by Spirit each step of the way. We follow the scent of our instincts towards the heart's awakening. Opening to the unknown takes faith

---

[6] Thomas Merton, *New Seeds of Contemplation* (New York: New Directions Publishing, 1961), 75.

and presence moment after moment. The mystery of God is experienced only by participation.

THE SEVENTH INVITATION – GRATITUDE

Gratitude enriches the soil in which Divine love grows. As our heart awakens to unity and connection, gratefulness flows. When the loving soul gazes into the eternal mirror, we can hear the words of Mechthild of Magdeburg, "Lord, between you and me all things are beautiful."[7] As our heart awakens to the mutuality of Divine love, the trajectory of our life shifts. We find ourselves enjoying our love relationship with God—walking through the park, sitting in the car together traveling to work, gazing at each other in the silence of night and basking in gratitude for the intimacy unfolding. We spread out in the sweetness that seeps into the sublime and the ordinary, and hear the call to gratefulness, the psalms of thanksgiving throughout our lives.

Being in Relationship

To be human is to be in relationship with self, others, and all of creation. We do not and cannot live alone, even if we're on a remote mountaintop. Relationships are living organisms, like flowers, requiring care and attention. They dwell at the very core of our being. I've learned about Divine love

---

[7] Mechthild of Magdeburg, *The Flowing Light of the Godhead*, trans. Frank Tobin, Classics of Western Spirituality (Mahwah, NJ: Paulist Press, 1997), 119.

through relations with my deepest self, my husband, siblings, parents, friends, colleagues, neighbors, those I see for spiritual direction, and the Earth herself.

Like all relationships, our connection with the Divine flourishes with love and attention. God invites us every day to come closer and closer, and as we do, we touch the root of all our relationships and taste what it means to trust.

How to Use This Book

I wrote *The Divine Heart* for you to use in any way that serves you. It can be a book to pray with, to leaf through its pages while you're on retreat, or to use as a source of reflections to share in community. There are seven chapters, each an invitation that can lead to a more intimate relationship with God, yourself, and others.

You might want to read the book all the way through and discover what stirs in you, or pray with each invitation for a week, a month, or longer before moving on to the next. We are all on a journey and need different things at different times. Listen to the still, small voice within and honor its message and gift of resonance.

Please approach each invitation as an exploration, a finger pointing to the ineffable, while allowing your heart to open and bloom in God's abiding love. My hope is that this small book will help you awaken, little by little, to God's love, to grow in it and learn to dwell in the joys and pleasures it brings.

Each invitation shines light on the connection between intimacy with the Divine and intimacy in daily life, and is supported by reflections, texts, prayer suggestions, and journaling encouragement. As you write your experiences down, your journal might become a personal prayer book, filled with questions, reflections, and supplications that might serve as markers along your sacred journey.

The Divine Heart offers ways to come to know the Divine as an intimate relationship, your daily companion, the ground from which all relationships deepen and grow. Awakening to this intimate companionship reveals how *home* is our heart, our rose, the place in God where we are called friend, embraced as fully as sunlight fills the sky. This is the limitless bounty of love.

There are no prerequisites. No degrees, lineage, or credentials are needed. There is no perfect discipline, nor does any one person or approach hold the key for you to enter this relationship and receive God's love. No one else can open the door to your heart, and no outsider is gatekeeper. Only God; only your deepest Self. We each enter this intimate relationship with the Divine in our own way. We're all born with an inner knowing, an indwelling Spirit, and we are always participating in God's love through our very lives.

This relationship has known me my entire life. Union with God is my origin; yet, at the same time, I'm constantly discovering, awakening, and allowing this sublime *something* to reveal itself. It's a mystery that knows me so deeply, it's intertwined with the strands of my hair, the ones I pull back and braid, then let loose to brush against my cheeks.

I long wondered, *What will teach me how to be in an intimate relationship with the Divine?* And now I know. It's my heart, God's Spirit, and silence. I must be as receptive as Mary was at the moment of the Immaculate Conception—fully open, available, and willing, filled with the power of "yes" and a trust in unfolding grace and intimacy. I know I must never stop praying and do my best to live in a state of prayer.

Cultivating a relationship with the Divine is a personal journey, yet not solely interior. It also reaches out to the world and opens like the petals of a rose. It is the love story we're all living. I never cease to be astonished by it.

Keeping a Journal

Taking time to keep a journal can deepen your intentions and integrate your experiences.

Journaling can help you observe and give form to your own unfolding relationship with the Divine—sensations, images, and thoughts that might, at first, seem ephemeral. If you'd like to keep a spiritual journal, here are some tips.

Select a format you like: The size, shape, paper, and binding should please you. Find a blank book that feels comfortable and inviting. Then select drawing and writing tools you like—pens, pencils, markers, pastels, crayons. I recommend you take them out of their packages and keep them handy on a tray.

Find a place to keep your journal: To integrate journaling into your daily life, it can help to keep your journal in a place that is easy to access—on a table, a bookshelf, a desk—so you can write or draw in it at any time of day.

Make a commitment: To honor your intention to journal—to remember and integrate your ongoing relationship with God—you need to make time for it, even a few minutes a day. Making time is, I believe, the most important item on the list. For many, it helps to make writing a ritual. I write first thing in the morning along with my cup of tea. In addition to the importance of the sacred and mundane content, frequency and ritualizing can contribute to the experience.

Follow the prompts in this book (and elsewhere) that inspire you: Always allow inspiration to be your guide. Only respond to the prompts that speak to you. Draw and write. By *drawing*, I mean making marks on the page—lines, shapes, or colors, whatever comes through you. They might have symbolic meaning, or they might mean nothing at all, just something that came through your hands and your heart.

Begin each session with a ritual: You can light a candle, make a cup of tea, say a prayer, or connect with your breath in a few moments of silence. The process of journaling and journeying is yours, and if you find ways to make these sacramental, it will encourage your Spirit to open and integrate your experiences of the Divine as they unfold.

Claim the Love Story You Were Born to Live

We're all created *from* and *for* love. Being in the flow of God's love is, for me, the very purpose of life. As a spiritual director who companions people on their search for deeper connection with Divine love, I've learned to be fully present as we discover sacredness in the struggles and joys of our daily lives. I've sat with women and men of many faith traditions and those with none at all, each sincerely desiring a relationship with the Divine, and I honor all their experiences. We are all loved, and profoundly worthy of love.

Love is a *becoming*—an experience, not a static phenomenon. It is in perpetual flow, something we can experience in the ordinary and nitty-gritty details of our lives. I invite you to join me on a journey toward ever-increasing intimacy with the Divine, to delighting fully in its fragrance and warmth, touching the sweet nectar at its core, and stepping into this Divine love in every aspect of your life. This is where we belong. It is our true home. This journey isn't linear, but circular, and as our heart opens, mutual intimacy deepens. Our longing for God and God's longing for us becomes one—the experience becomes reciprocal. Claim the love story you were born to live. Enter and deepen this birthright of your relationship with the Divine—with the intimacy of God's love.

THE FIRST INVITATION: RECEPTIVITY

LISTENING AND RESPONDING

"You must have a capacity to receive,
or even omnipotence can't give."

— C. S. LEWIS [1]

For most of my life, I've felt encouraged to give. As a woman, a Catholic who was raised in a large family, I've always had an orientation toward giving. And deep in my heart I want to give—it feels right and comes naturally to me.

Yet it bears remembering that giving is the true and worthy partner of *receiving*. As vessels of the Divine, love flows into us and out of us, creating "the love of God [that] has been poured into our hearts by the Holy Spirit which has

---

1 C. S. Lewis, *A Grief Observed* (San Francisco: HarperOne, 2001), 46.

been given us."[2] Giving and receiving go hand in hand. They coexist. Thus, the love we give is love we've received from God. We learn and inherit love from the Divine.

The Divine longs for us to receive this gift of pure love, and it is God that initiates this relationship. In Genesis, God breathes the breath of life into us, and we become living souls. In Exodus, God speaks to Moses from the burning bush in an act of faithful love. In the Gospel of Matthew, God invites Mary to become the Holy Mother. God loves the world so much "that God sends his only Son," St. John tells us, and we are invited to receive Him.

In my book, *Seeking Surrender: How My Friendship with a Trappist Monk Taught Me to Trust and Embrace Life*,[3] I described a time of letting go and receiving Divine love even more fully. As my husband and I faced not being able to conceive, my sister slipping away with cancer, and my husband struggling with the need to close his small business, the Divine held me in the strong hand of infinite love. Throughout times of loss and sorrow, I've experienced the profound tenderness of God's love. God became the warm water with which I washed my tear-stained face, a softness caressing my aching body, and a compassionate presence that filled the hole in my heart.

Along the journey from grief to grace to surrender, my relationship to Divine love has expanded and grown, and

---

[2] Romans 5:3-8 (NRSV).
[3] Colette Lafia, *Seeking Surrender: How My Friendship with a Trappist Monk Taught Me to Trust and Embrace Life* (Notre Dame, IN: Sorin Books, 2015).

I've found new depths of intimacy within. While the stark contrasts of emptiness and wholeness unfolded before and within me, I began to ponder if I could learn to dwell even more completely in this great and abiding love.

My search began with the question, *How do I let God love me more, so our relationship can deepen?* I rolled the words around in my mouth like a piece of hard candy until slowly, it began to dissolve. I asked my mother, my spiritual director, and finally Brother Paul Quenon, a monk at the Abbey of Gethsemane in Kentucky. Brother Paul and I were walking through the woods one cool afternoon after visiting Thomas Merton's cinderblock hermitage. I stayed close as he identified the many birdcalls we were hearing. Finally, I said, "Can I ask you something?"

"Sure," he stated, happily.

"How do I let God love me more?"

Without missing a beat, Brother Paul answered in his joyful tone, "God *cannot* love you more. God already loves you infinitely. You just need to become more aware of His love."

"How?" I asked, with childlike curiosity.

"By becoming more present to it. It's like hearing birdcalls. By paying attention and delighting in it."

With Brother Paul's wisdom etched in my mind, I prayed to be more receptive to the landscape of love within my heart and all around me, recognizing that I was already in a love relationship with the Divine, as are you.

We tend to hold back and resist, afraid we'll lose ourselves in the vast unknown. Can you stay present with your resistance, get to know it, befriend it, and accept it? Its message is deep and personal. What is it trying to protect you from? Make a relationship with that as well.

In our journey towards a deeper and more abiding love relationship with the Divine, we grow by encountering and understanding our barriers. At the same time, stay open to the glimmerings of God's grace that you *can* feel, see, or intuit. As you surrender to all aspects of your inner knowing, grace, *and* resistance, you'll enter into a fuller relationship with God's boundless love.

How do we make *receptivity* a foundation of our relationship with the Divine and of our life of prayer? To give love, we also need to be able to receive it. This invitation to receptivity encourages us to listen to the stirrings of love, release into communion with God, and become more present to Divine love. "God cannot love you more. God already loves you infinitely." Embracing this love, we can respond to God, others, and all of life from our heart, which is the source of compassion toward all.

1. Be Willing to Engage in Deep Listening

> Let me hear what God the Lord will speak,
> for he will speak peace to his people,
> to his faithful, to those who turn to
> him in their hearts...[4]

---

[4] Psalms 85:8 (NRSV).

Listen is the first word in the prologue of *The Rule*, the guidelines for Christian monastics composed by St. Benedict 1,500 years ago: *Listen carefully, my child, to my instructions, and attend to them with the ear of your heart.*[5]

From church towers to meditation halls all around the world, the sounds of bells call us to listen, to be attentive and become present to the Divine within and around us. We're invited to trust in this call, have faith in this Great Voice, and awaken to the Divine love that is there awaiting us. As Buddhist monk and teacher Thich Nhat Hanh has said, "To love is to listen."[6]

The core of my training as a spiritual director focuses on the art and practice of contemplative listening, learning to hear the Spirit at work in a person's life with the "ear of [the] heart." We learn to notice and be attentive; to honor silence and respond to what's taking place in a person's body, mind, and spirit. We listen to God's call with our whole selves. We listen into the stillness of fresh snow and the clamor of pounding rain. We slow down and let ourselves discover what our heart already hears. In deep listening, we're called to be a part of the presence of God in the world.

We're in great company on the journey of listening. When God told Joseph in a dream not to fear taking pregnant Mary as his wife, Joseph listened.[7] When God told the

---

[5] Joan Chittister, *The Rule of Benedict: A Spirituality for the 21st Century* (New York: The Crossroad Publishing Company, 2010), 3.
[6] Offered by Thich Nhat Hanh during a retreat the author attended at Mount Madonna Center, Watsonville, California, c. 1996.
[7] Matthew 1:20 (NRSV).

three wise men not to return to Herod and tell him where the Christ child was, they listened.[8] When God called to the prophet Samuel, with the counsel of Eli, he heard the Lord and said, "Speak, for your servant is listening."[9]

God speaks to us in our actual lives, sometimes in surprising ways: a gull flying high in the sky, a flash on a crowded bus, a rose on a bedroom dresser. These messages come without warning, and the more grounded we are in Divine love, the more these experiences can awaken us to a life in the Spirit. These are raw moments of grace—gifts we can receive if we listen to the stirring in our hearts.

Last year on New Year's Day, I sat in front of the fireplace staring into the flames and listening to the rain tapping on the living room windows. My shoulders were hunched over, my mind troubled. Over and over, I reviewed problems at work, financial pressures, a series of worries. As I poured my heart and tears out to God, three words sprung up inside of me: *Live in hope.*

I'm not generally a hopeful person, a habit formed growing up in a large household with an alcoholic mother, watching things get worse day after day for seven years. These words from a wellspring deep within stopped me in my tracks. They surprised me the way a bright yellow flower on the tip of a desert cactus might. They were unfamiliar to my usual way of approaching life yet felt like an invitation: *Live in hope.*

---

[8] Matthew 2:12 (NRSV).
[9] 1 Samuel 3:10 (NRSV).

How do we trust unexpected moments when we hear words that sound incongruent and unfamiliar? First, we notice them: the words, sensations, images, stirrings in our hearts and dreams, and the deep silence that often follows. Something draws us in, and we stop and listen.

In moments like this, feeling the effect of these words on my heart, I prayed: What does it mean for me right now, *to live in hope?* I wasn't sure. Listening requires faith, discernment, and patience, staying open to what we don't yet grasp and allowing the creative tension. Was I willing to let these words enter me?

Slowly, I began to understand that to live in hope means to trust that I'm not alone; that I am in a *togetherness* with God. I was being invited—again through my heart—into a dynamic relationship with the Divine that was unfurling in ways I could never have predicted or planned. Listening, I got closer to God, and God came closer to me.

As we cultivate our receptivity to God and Self, we begin to listen more deeply to others. When my husband tells me, his voice strained, his sense of self bruised, about a pay reduction at work, I listen with an open heart and as Thomas Merton wrote, "become doors and windows through which God shines back into His own house."[10]

There are times we fail to listen or become reactive, resistant, or turn away, but we can learn to persevere, to trust that whatever we lack God will supply—if we ask. Cultivating a receptive heart takes time, and some awakenings seem

---

[10] Merton, *New Seeds*, 67.

subtle. But through prayer, devotion, and growing awareness, our ability to listen with our heart becomes stronger.

FROM MY SPIRITUAL JOURNAL

> *Let me be one who receives love. The eight-year-old in me*
> *needing to lean into a warm hug; the twenty-year-old filled*
> *with passion; the forty-year-old yearning and seeking her*
> *own way; the fifty-year-old loving with a longer lens on*
> *life. I touch the need for God's tender love at every turn, in*
> *every period of my life. I need it—like breath, sunlight, and*
> *water—to live. I feel my tears, the spiritual gems that hold*
> *my trust and tenderness.*

PRAYERS AND PRACTICES

1. I like to begin with what I call the "Heart Prayer."
   Begin by taking a few conscious breaths and
   becoming receptive to God's love pouring into you,
   moment after moment. Close your eyes and dwell
   in this love for five minutes, or more if you'd like.
   Imagine yourself a rose being watered at the roots.
2. Write and/or draw in your journal about a time you
   felt you were listening with the "ear of your heart."
   This might have been an experience in nature, a
   moment with a loved one, in prayer, or within your
   deepest self.
3. Take a *listening walk*. Really listen to the sounds that
   come in and out of awareness—a bird's song, the

whoosh of the wind, your shoes making contact
with the pavement. Become receptive to the sounds
around you, even ones you usually think of as
unpleasant. Can you hear the stirring of the Divine?

2. Be Willing to Release

Our desire for more intimacy with the Divine helps us
release into this love. By letting go of our stubborn sense of
separateness, we make more space for God, and others. We
free ourselves from the constant desire to be different, "other
than," or special. We come to honor our uniqueness *and* the
uniqueness of others in a way that genuinely values us and
each created being. We release into a true sense of belonging, our interconnectedness with all of life—to a star in the
sky, a leaf on a tree, a kiss on a check. Each of us is distinct,
and at the same time we're a part of the whole. As we learn
to listen more deeply to ourselves and others, we experience a unity with God, others, and all of creation, and we
recognize the dynamic flow of life and love we are a part of.

After twenty-five years of marriage, I have learned that
when two people come together, a new entity is born. An *us*
is created. The other person is not the object of our love, but
love itself, and it is through union that we experience love.
We walk our individual paths, at the same time releasing
ourselves into a deeper union, allowing a sacred bond to
grow and transform us.

We come together in hope of living what Martin Buber

called the I-Thou relationship, in which "we relate with the entirety of our being to another whole person. It is more than a way of relating to others; it is also how we can, a bit at a time, experience God's presence in the world."[11]

I remember the words of Brother Bartholomew, another Trappist monk I met at Gethsemane, as he drove me from the monastery to the airport. He said that living a life of God is like playing basketball—we constantly need to throw the ball into God's hands. We can't hold onto the ball. When he dropped me off, he smiled with his royal blue eyes and reminded me, "Keep throwing the ball to God." Releasing what we're holding and giving ourselves to God are constant and immediate. Each day we pray, I offer my life to You.

As we give ourselves to God more fully and keep releasing ourselves into the wholeness of love, we experience Divine love breathing into us, and although this deepening happens gradually, we learn to "trust in the slow work of God," as philosopher and priest Teilhard de Chardin taught.[12] We inevitably will meet our inner storms and lingering shadows: the voices filled with doubt and self-attack. But the more awareness we gain, the more we trust that God *is* our shelter in the storm, our rock, our shield, our strength. Through prayer and meditation, we learn to stay steady as the hurricane winds blow. As the Psalm declares, "Be still

---

[11] myjewishlearning.com/article/i-and-thou-selected-passages, trans. Walter Kaufmann.
[12] Quoted in Michael Harter, *Hearts on Fire: Praying with Jesuits* (Chicago: Loyola Press, 2005), 38.

and know that I am God."[13] Grace is always with us, and the consciousness we are living in communion with the Divine cannot help but deepen and grow.

When we become more aware of God in us, as subtle as that is at times, we dare open our hearts and step in over the seeming cracks of imperfection, ideals, and conflicting ideas of who we believe we—or God—should be. As we become more reflective, we gain self-knowledge and notice the edges of fear, self-criticism, doubt, and repetitive thought patterns. St. Teresa of Avila wrote to her nuns, "I do not know if I have explained this clearly: self-knowledge is so important that, even if you were raised right up to the heavens, I should like you to never stop your cultivation of it..."[14]

Step by step, we become receptive to God's invitation to release our constricted selves into the capacious heart of the Divine, where our wholeness and connection commune with love and life. It is here that the voice of love brings compassion. We turn *toward* the love, which is pouring into us, releasing our heart more freely as we respond to God's great generosity.

FROM MY SPIRITUAL JOURNAL

> *I release all that I am into the hem of God, skin to skin, breath to breath, desire to desire. I am fabric; make me*

---

[13] Psalms 46:10 (NRSV).
[14] Teresa of Avila, "First Mansions, Chapter 1," in *Interior Castle*, trans. E. Allison Peers (New York: Image Books/Doubleday, 1989), 23.

into your garment. I am flour; make me into your bread. I am Your breath, breathe me. I give myself to you, my God. Full of abandon, I'm touching a love that will carry me over mountains. And I know that unless I give myself away, nothing can happen.

PRAYERS AND PRACTICES

1. Sit in a comfortable position and take several deep breaths. Feel your spine like the stem of a flower reaching upward. Feel the breath flowing in and out of your body. Let your breath bring you a sense of connection to the source of all life, Divine love.

2. Pray with the words, *I offer my life to You.* Let the words sink into your heart. Repeat them several times slowly. Breathe into them.

3. In your journal, explore what it means for you to offer your life to God. You may try drawing what this looks and feels like or find an image that reflects this for you and paste it into your journal.

3. Be Willing to Be Present to Divine Love

As we learn to listen deeply and release ourselves, we become more sensitive and aware of God's inseparable presence from us—how God lives in us, and we live in God. And in the presence of this Presence, we come home to ourselves. Paradoxically, we must also be willing to be present to ourselves, to the Self that exists in God. We are like the rose that cannot force growth but is completely receptive to the life it's destined to live, blooming in God into its fulfillment and purpose.

We can discover the presence of God in our hearts—and our hearts in God—by sitting still with a heart that is quiet, attentive, and mindful. In this state of receptivity, we recognize and acknowledge communion with the Divine and allow God's presence to fill all the corners of our being. We experience a melding, a natural union; "Our life and God's life are one intimate life," as contemplative teacher James Finley said in a talk at the Living School.[15] With a trustful heart and a prayer for grace, we enter this sacred place of togetherness.

In *The Little Prince*, by Antoine de Saint-Exupéry, the fox asks the Little Prince to become his friend. The Little Prince says he needs to know how to do this, so the fox tells him, "You must be very patient. First you will sit down at a little distance from me—like this—in the grass. I shall look at you out of the corner of my eye, and you will say nothing...but you will sit a little closer to me, every day..."[16]

In a similar way, our relationship with God strengthens, with patience and steadiness, from tentative attention and devotion to increasingly consistent trust and confidence. As our desire for a more intimate relationship with God grows,

[15] Offered by James Finley during the Living School Symposium, August 6-10, 2017.
[16] Antoine de Saint-Exupéry, *The Little Prince* (Boston: Mariner Books, 2000).

we allow God to draw us closer and commit ourselves to being in this intimate relationship and being known completely. We have faith in the promise of love.

We will each find the unique way our heart opens to this constant love, this Divine presence, if we listen *with* our hearts, *in* our hearts, and *through* our hearts, remaining deeply present to ourselves. We can extend this receptivity by the way we respond to the people in our lives, and in the process, become more intimate with God.

A few years ago, my husband and I faced a crossroads in our marriage. I was in my early fifties, feeling burdened by financial pressures and aching to work less. I was frustrated about monetary decisions we'd made—not saving much for retirement, my husband working as an independent consultant rather than for an established firm, my decision to work part-time in education, refinancing our mortgage and not having a plan to pay it down.

Since my teens, I've felt the stress to earn money, swirling cones in a yogurt shop, serving popcorn in a theater, nannying to get through college. Later I worked as an elementary school teacher, a grant writer for a nonprofit, a development consultant for educators, and then a school librarian. My income was never enough, and the pressures inside me were now volcanic.

One dark night, after my husband and I argued loudly and hurtfully, I sat on the sofa stiff and worn out. My husband came over and said to me, "I can't live like this—you have to ask yourself if you can accept our lives as they are."

He said it with such honesty and clarity that his words cracked me open.

I brought my lack of acceptance to spiritual direction, and with the help of my spiritual director, I was able to unravel the tangle of feelings and realize that I wasn't living from the depth of my heart. I was stuck on the surface, angry about the past. Was I capable of tuning in to the great movement of love in my life: a deeper sense of marriage and commitment to my husband, myself, and God?

I took time each morning before work to journal, draw, and pray, and at the end of each day, I cried out to God like in the Psalms, "Relieve the anguish in my heart, and set me free from my distress."[17] Slowly, I felt a tap on my shoulder to enter another room, one that was more spacious. I was being invited to listen and live a deeper union with my husband as the sacred other. We were anchored in Divine love—I could feel it—our union connected at the root to the Source of love. Did I have faith in love's promise?

A few days later, my husband and I talked again.

"I need you to have faith in me as I work to regain faith in myself," I told him. "I love you. I need you to understand that I'm going through so many changes in my body and in my psyche," I said.

He shared that he too was going through a transition, coming to terms with himself and trying to accept his own journey. Some days, he said, were easier than others.

As we talked, our voices softened.

---

[17] Psalms 25 (NRSV).

"Let's cut each other some slack," he said.

"Let's give each other more compassion," I added.

We came back to a togetherness, a place of faith in our marriage, and a commitment to be good stewards of our life together. We were sharing a financial responsibility and the pressures of making and saving money, and at the same time, we wanted to honor our creative desires and personal needs.

In the midst of chaos and darkness, we chose to stay present to the flow of the love between us. We chose to listen from the heart. *This is the wisdom of receptivity.* We were invited to tune in to the unfurling petals of the Divine within each of us. We became grateful for the way God's teachings about listening and responding had shaped our relationship.

FROM MY SPIRITUAL JOURNAL

> *I must not stay behind the gate, closed off within myself;*
> *rather I must open the latch and follow my longing. Divine*
> *Presence is in everything. I am living in a world soaked*
> *and saturated with love. I follow this urge as I'm sitting*
> *on the subway; working at my desk; enveloped in my*
> *husband's bold embrace—this love always present in my*
> *beating heart.*

PRAYERS AND PRACTICES

1. Gently place your hand over your heart and repeat the mantra: *I'm at home in myself,* as you sink more and more into yourself. Add the mantra: *God is at home in me.* Close your eyes if you'd like, and take it all in.
2. In your journal, write about the ways your heart is a home for God. Use the prompt, "My heart is a home for the Divine, because it is..." You might add a drawing of what this feels like.
3. Engage in being a contemplative presence for others—being still, attentive, and heart-centered. Listen without giving advice or interrupting—give the person space and time, your full presence and receptivity.

CLOSING REFLECTIONS

When we really listen, the sounds wash over us—cries, whispers, the wind howling, the closing of a door, ocean waves crashing on the beach. In silence, a heart beats, salt pours from its shaker, a hand takes another in its grasp.

As I'm held in this constant vibration of sounds and silence, I listen and feel for the holy and sacred in every note, pulse, and pause, attentive to their presence in the open field of my heart. I sense what I cannot find words for; I touch what so quickly disappears. God needs room to be heard, and my soul needs room to hear what dwells in the lining of my being. "Hush," I remind myself. "Listen to the soles of the ballet slippers crossing the wooden floor."

There is a way of listening *with* God; a shared listening that takes place when we hear from the heart. We allow our heart to open and take the lead. We step aside, "Please, after you," opening the gate with sincerity and entering into God within. Listening from the heart is compassionate. We reveal ourselves in the depth of intimate listening, and the thin, paper-doll images of ourselves slip away. This is the tenderness of God's love.

It has taken me a lifetime of listening to realize how much the Holy One is on my side; to become present to what my elderly mother told me, "God is available twenty-four hours a day; you don't need an appointment." This presence of God permeates all we do. We hear God reminding us, *I'm always with you, in this kiss, this pain, this joy, this restlessness.* We're called inside, into the rosebud of our hearts, to make room for this listening; for this presence in our lives.

☙

Further Journal Exploration

Listen to psalms to deepen the quality of receptivity in your relationship with God. Read aloud slowly from several psalms. Which words speak to you? Which are the ones the heart hears?

from Psalms 27: 7-9

Hear, O Lord, when I cry aloud,
be gracious to me and answer me!
"Come," my heart says, "seek his face!"
Your face, Lord do I seek.
Do not hide your face from me.

from Psalms 34: 4-7

I sought the Lord, and he answered me,
and delivered me from all my fears.
Look to him, and be radiant;
so your faces shall never be ashamed.
The poor soul cried, and was heard
by the Lord,
and was saved from every trouble.

from Psalms 85: 8

Let me hear what God the Lord will speak,
for he will speak peace to his people,
to his faithful, to those who turn to him
in their hearts.

JOURNAL PROMPTS

Let the Spirit be your guide. Feel free to respond only to what speaks to you in the moment.

- Write down words or phrases from any of these psalms that touch your heart.
- Read them slowly, and perhaps aloud.
- Take one or a few words and begin writing or drawing. See what happens. What's stirring inside you?
- Create a prayer of listening, using the prompt: I *will listen to...*

End with a few minutes of silence, grateful for taking time to be with yourself and listening from the heart.

THE SECOND INVITATION: DELIGHT

FEELING LIFE'S WONDERS, SAVORING EACH MOMENT

"Every Object, Every Being is a jar full of delight."
— RUMI

When I was ten, I spent most of the summer at the local pool, swimming for hours, holding my breath underwater for as long as I could, and diving off the high board. I climbed up the metal ladder filled with anticipation, my ten-year-old toes tingling, my heart racing. I'd arch forward with my arms extended and knees slightly bent, and dive into the clear, blue water.

I dove hundreds of times that summer, each time as wondrous as the last. I was delighted by the freedom of leaping into the air, the trust and confidence I found in myself, and the feeling of the water taking me in. When we delight in something, we're filled with wonder and allow each moment to embrace us with endless possibilities. We taste life's gifts and savor our newfound joy.

Diving freely into life is one way to experience God's *delight*, and to join in God knowing who we are, "For the Lord delights in his people."[1] The way I felt diving from the high board was also the delight God shared with me as my body plunged, sleek as an arrow, into the waiting water.

Can we trust that God is already delighting in us? It's not something we need to earn or make happen with effort, but rather something we can *allow*. Our habit is to control our lives; yet this is a time to let go, to trust our desire to know and love God more, to delight in our union. This is a journey of the heart, stripping away its protective coat and becoming free to absorb God's love, a joy that emanates and flows from the core of love. This delight awakens our hearts and invites us into a more creative, dynamic, abundant relationship with God, others, our deepest self, and all of creation.

That God delights in, through, and with us was, for me, a stunning realization. A few years ago, while facilitating a retreat on *Women in Transition* at Mercy Center in Burlingame, California, I placed a selection of images—nature photographs, reproductions of paintings, calendar pictures—on a long table and invited participants to select an image that represented their feelings or their inner selves during this time of transition in their lives. I surprised myself when I

---

[1] Psalms 149:4 (NIV).

chose a photo of a wolf with a thick beige-and-black coat walking alone out of a snow-covered forest.

That image continued to speak to me for over a year. In prayer, it grew stronger, and I began to sense God's presence in the image with me. Then I heard the words, *You are a beautiful, wild thing; you are My creature,* and I could almost feel God rubbing my thick fur. I sensed Divine delight in a part of me I was only just discovering and accepting: my wildness and my beauty, inside and out.

Delight implores us to realize that we're God's beloveds. At first, we might shy away, feeling unworthy or "not enough," dubious it could be possible. But love is love; and God's love has no conditions. The more we awaken to delight, the more abundant it becomes in our lives.

As we allow the presence of Spirit to be our daily guide, and as we begin to recognize, appreciate, and connect to the gifts of creation, we let God take the lead.

> I cannot dance, O Lord,
> Unless You lead me.
> If You wish me to leap joyfully,
> Let me see You dance and sing—
> — Mechthild of Magdeburg[2]

How do we *delight* in Divine presence and in the constant surprises of creation? As the way of delight awakens in our lives, we learn to engage more fully with what's already around us, to feel wonder and savor the moments

---

[2] Hirshfield, *Beguine Spirituality,* 86.

of our life, the joy in our heart. We can learn to live in God's generosity, knowing God is with us, here and now.

1. Engaging with What's Around Us

The Benedictine monk and author David Steindl-Rast writes, "God's inexhaustible poetry comes to me in five languages: seeing, hearing, smelling, touching and tasting." He tells us that there's a divine poetry of sensuousness, and that the outside and inside, the external and internal, are of one piece. "We must learn to really see with our eyes so that we begin to look with our heart also,"[3] he writes.

Today, I awaken under cotton sheets as the golden morning light peers in through the bedroom curtains. *Dear God, thank you for bringing me to this new day.* Once out of bed, I wash my face, feeling the warm water caress my waking skin. I make a full-bodied cup of English breakfast tea, with milk and sugar, and the first sip, as always, feels like a gift. I hear birds trilling and tweeting from my open bedroom window, bringing a smile to my lips. *They, too, are starting their day. We're all busy and joyous!* My senses invite me into a place of gratitude and awareness.

At the school library where I work, the day is filled with the sounds of children—their laughter, cries, and shouts of excitement. My senses awaken me to all that's around me, inviting me to connect with and delight in others. The day winds down with a swim at the local pool, and for an hour,

---

[3] gratefulness.org/resource/encounter-god-senses.

I'm enveloped by cool water splashing over me. As evening is ushered in, my husband and I prepare dinner, filling the kitchen with the earthy aroma of potatoes roasting in the oven.

Our senses connect us to creation; everything we see, taste, hear, smell, and touch becomes a moment of union reflecting God's glory. "Listen, open a window to God and begin to delight yourself by gazing upon Him through the opening," the poet Rumi proclaimed.[4]

We find delight engaging our senses, reframing our experiences, allowing in the abundance already around us. Moments of delight are intimate, joyful, and playful. They're my husband and I laughing together before drifting off to sleep; my ninety-year-old mother hugging me, touching my salt-and-pepper hair and remarking how lovely I look; or bursting out singing while riding along on my bicycle. These are embodied moments when we're touched and awakened by the truth that we're never separated from creation and the infinite generosity of God's love.

These moments invite us into intimacy with ourselves and the life of the senses. The inner draws the outer to itself, as we open more to God's presence in our lives. We accept this invitation by engaging with the world as a holy place of depth and texture, rather than dismissing it as profane or taking it for granted. As Julian of Norwich, the

---

[4] *Jewels of Remembrance: A Daybook of Spiritual Guidance Containing 365 Selections from the Wisdom of Rumi,* trans. Camille Adams Helminski and Kabir Helminski (Boulder, CO: Shambhala Publications, 2000), 172.

fourteenth-century mystic, tells us, "The fullness of joy is to contemplate God in everything."[5]

When our senses feel overwhelmed, even assaulted, we may need to withdraw to a quiet place and allow in silence to restore our balance. That too is an invitation to enter the realm of God intimately. Our senses are still with us as we delight in simplicity and emptiness.

From the senses to the soul, and from the soul to the senses, we experience and connect with God's love, which is creative and overflowing, pouring forth tirelessly. We declare, "My soul is satisfied as with a rich feast, and my mouth praises you with joyful lips."[6] The more we pay full attention to the boundless flow of delight, the more we're willing to discover all the ways that God, life, and all of creation are constantly surprising us with gifts. We attune our ears to the words of God, who is always saying to us, *You have been created in Love; Your essence is Love. I delight in you.* If we allow ourselves to truly feel and experience with our senses, we'll find ourselves in the garden of delight every day—in a landscape of abundance filled with praise. As delight grows in us, true joy emerges.

FROM MY SPIRITUAL JOURNAL

> *There is another way. To live in this pouring out; to laugh and stick my tongue out in the rain. I am filled with desire.*

---

[5] Julian of Norwich, *Showings*, trans. Edmund Colledge and James Walsh, Classics of Western Spirituality (Mahwah, NJ: Paulist Press, 1978), 237.
[6] Psalms 63:3-5 (NRSV).

> *The sun rises and takes me into its brilliance and glory.*
> *I enter the dome of surprise. Mother of Mothers, keep me*
> *seeing more; let me be the thread of your thread. Creation*
> *is perpetual, infinite engagement. I wish to compose life in*
> *broad strokes and fine details, in symphonies and silence.*
> *I notice the little holy flowers growing in the cracks of the*
> *sidewalk.*

PRAYERS AND PRACTICES

1. Begin by quietly praying with Julian's powerful words, "The fullness of joy is to behold God in everything." Repeat the words until they enter your heart deeply.
2. In your journal, write about your day through the experiences of your senses—the crunchy peanut butter on your toast, the breeze through an open window, the shining smile of someone you meet. Allow the list to become a prayer of joy and gratitude for what's present in your life.
3. Take time to read one of the creation stories in the Book of Genesis, and ask yourself: *How am I a part of creation?*

2. Filled with Wonder

Children are intuitively drawn to stories with wonder, curiosity, and joy. To them, a dancing pig wearing a wig is hilarious; an imaginary friend named Beekle looking for a child to belong to causes their warm hearts to glow; and a lonely goldfish that finally gets another fish put into his bowl completely satisfies their longing for connection. Children marvel at the natural world, at the seventeen species of penguins, the lifecycle of a butterfly, and the numerous names for apples like Winesap, Mutsu, and Pink Lady. I always enjoy reading stories to children.

How do we hear the invitation to enjoy God more in our lives and become more playful? God wants to increase our playfulness and through our playfulness, our joy. An ascent is being offered to us, as described in the words of Meister Eckhart: "Know then that my soul is as young as when she was created, in fact much younger! And I tell you, I should be ashamed if she were not much younger tomorrow than today!"[7]

So many possibilities begin with the simple words *I wonder*. I wonder how a rose can have so many petals. I wonder how I can love so much. I wonder at the color of red beets and the brilliant patterns of tropical fish. I wonder at the Divine's infinite love for each and every one of us. Wonder is an extension of curiosity, and curiosity and awe are the lifeblood of delight.

During a time when I felt drained and needed inspiration, I wondered if I might enjoy painting, so I signed up for a weekly art class. I bought a set of acrylic paints, a roll

---

[7] *Meister Eckhart: The Essential Writings*, trans. Raymond B. Blakney (New York: Harper, 1957), 134, adapted by Karsten Harries.

of canvas, and a few brushes. I had no expectations, having never painted before, but I was curious, looking to discover what I didn't know.

I liked the instructor immediately. She was in her late sixties, wore a vibrant orange blouse, and carried herself with ease and self-possession. In her opening remarks, she boldly stated, "Creativity is like a faucet, just waiting to flow. All we need is to allow ourselves to turn it on." Our first assignment was to paint how we were feeling, using memory and imagination. For three uninterrupted hours, I painted, stroke after stroke, color on color. Something was guiding my brush, something that knew what to do. The instructor gave me space to explore what was moving in me onto the canvas, and she left me alone.

As I painted, I felt the faucet open, and what had been dormant began to flow, just as she'd said. A voice in me kept saying *yes* with each mark, and I could sense the rise of delight. I painted a large mountain in shades of blue sitting against a purplish sky. Through painting freely, with child-like delight and curiosity, I felt I was touching God and God was touching me.

Delight is a way for us to share in the joy of creation, to discover the Divine and experience a deeper sense of wonder and connection. "Every creation is a little expression of God; every tree; every person; every little grain of sand," Ilia Delio, a theologian and Franciscan nun, reminds us.[8]

---

[8] Sr. Ilia Delio, *Christian Life: An Adventure in Love* (Washington, DC: Now You Know Media, 2009), audiobook.

Delight is a spiritual awareness, penetrating the heart of experience. In every moment, we're given an opportunity to discover and rediscover the infinite generosity of creation. We can choose to say *yes* and pray for the grace to inhabit it. We can attune our ears and hearts to hear the words in the creation story in Genesis, as though spoken to us directly: *And God said it was good.*

We are living the creation story. We are participating in it! We proclaim with the poet Mary Oliver, "I walk in the world to love it."[9] What a wonder!

There will be times we lose our sense of wonder, times when we hide and contract, feeling we're not enough. In those moments, we don't feel wondrous. Instead, we stare into the mirror of inadequacy.

A few years ago, I came across my late father's copy of *The Spiritual Exercises of Saint Ignatius of Loyola* that I had on my bookshelf. I pulled it from the shelf, opened the red cover, and found between the pages a note in my father's handwriting that said, "By your cross, Jesus, free me from past fantasies to control past events and people, to redo my life, for riches, fame, honor. Make me Your follower. Give me Deep Compassion." In that moment, I saw so clearly that I was doing the same thing to myself and my life. I wanted to redo the past. I was feeling disappointed that I hadn't achieved certain things, that I didn't measure up, that I wasn't enough.

---

[9] Mary Oliver, *Long Life: Essays and Other Writings* (Boston: Da Capo Press, 2005), 40.

I took his note and my aching heart to spiritual direction. Really, I was taking a long-held family story, one that had passed from generation to generation tinged with fear and shame. As I held my father's note, a thought pierced my heart, "I can't carry it anymore," and I began to cry. God heard my cry, and in that moment, I was released like a bird from a cage. I've revisited that moment many times since, asking for the grace and commitment to see myself as God's beloved and my life as more than a checklist of accomplishments.

God delights in our uniqueness as part of the creation of life. We're not only loved, we're God's wonder—our being, thumbprint, and laugh, the deep pools of our eyes and the longing of our hearts. Just as God delights in us, we're invited to celebrate all that surrounds us. Can you see yourself through the eyes of Divine love? Can you take that leap of faith? Through the spiritual awareness of delight, we recognize that we are living *in* the awe of creation and that our very existence *is* the spectacular gift of creation.

We're invited to become the miracle and marvel we were born to be, to see ourselves shimmering in God's light. As we ponder the unspoken stories of the stars, we say to ourselves in that midnight-black moment, *I am this. I am that. And then some.*

FROM MY SPIRITUAL JOURNAL

You, God, are bigger and bigger and bigger. I open the door, leaving a house that is too small for me, a place I cannot live in anymore. I offer my brokenness, my grief, my sadness, trusting everything can be used for my transformation in love. I wonder what's happening; I don't know. I'm in an oceanic love.

PRAYERS AND PRACTICES

1. Practice "Seeing Prayer." Simply look more deeply at things. Notice the colors, textures, and shapes of the strawberries at the breakfast table, the roses in the garden, the faces of those around you. Bring depth and delight to your seeing today.
2. Enter the space of *enough*, and find God waiting there, happy to see you. Practice the mantra, "I am enough. I've always been enough."
3. Engage in journal writing, using the prompt: *What do I wonder about?* Feel free to add some drawing to your response—in the simple form of colors, shapes, or lines.

3. Savoring

We can also find delight by savoring our experiences, allowing them to feel even more abundant. I learned the art of savoring from my late teacher and friend Leigh Hyams, an artist who experienced the world with her senses, as though it were a living painting. One summer, Leigh and I sat together in a café in San Miguel de Allende looking out an open window. It was 4:00 p.m., and the dusty streets were filling with shoppers. There we sat, sipping our hot chocolates and eating warm, chewy *churros* sprinkled with cinnamon.

Leigh leaned back into the painted cobalt blue chair and, lifting the clay mug to her lips, paused for a moment, inhaling the spicy Mexican chocolate before taking a sip. We lingered for a good hour in the café, delighting in the sights and sounds of this Mexican town she now called home after decades living in an artist's loft in San Francisco, where we met in my first painting class. I took a few more bites of my churros, my mouth buzzing with sugar. We laughed as she licked her fingers, sharing these moments of delight, allowing a natural, unspoken intimacy between us awaken and unfold.

We're more likely to connect to delightful moments when we remember to stop, recognize all that is good around us, and follow our instinct toward joy. We can learn to savor each moment, lingering and apprehending the world, finding union in a broken twig dipping into a jar of ink and making a mark on a fresh sheet of paper. God wants a pathway to our heart, and we want a path to the heart of God.

We can relate to life and connect to God out of abundance, not denial. We don't need to cut ourselves off from the lavish feast of love and creation that awaits us. In his book on St. John of the Cross, the Carmelite Iain Matthew dared to write, "But where God is concerned, the problem lies in our desiring too little, and growing means expanding our expectations; or rather, making [God's] generosity, not our poverty, the measure of our expectations."[10]

Being more present to our experiences is a way to *embody* the moments of delight in our lives. Delightful moments are embodied, and we are awakened to the truth that we are never separated from the spirit of creation and the infinite generosity of the love of God. From this mutuality, we can embrace ourselves, others, and all of creation. We stop and listen to the wind. We see the shapes of shadows on the sidewalk. We trust our instincts. We're filled with a longing that leads us to an even fuller experience of delight.

Noting our particular ways of being in the world, we recognize where and how we find delight. Some days, I like to linger as I fold towels. I meet what I'm doing with ease, sacred intention, and pleasure. I feel I'm together with God as I empty the laundry basket onto the bed and savor the sacrament of this moment. With each bend of my arms, I fold joy and delight into the experience. The sight of freshly laundered towels gives both my husband and me immense satisfaction. So many moments invite us to *"loafe and invite my soul,"* as Walt Whitman describes, to *"lean and loafe at my ease...observing a spear of summer grass."*[11]

We can delight in the unpredictable and surprising, grace-filled ways God shows up in our daily lives, drinking a mug of hot chocolate, folding a basketful of clean towels,

---

[10] Iain Matthew, *The Impact of God: Soundings from St. John of the Cross* (London: Hodder & Stoughton, 1995), 33.
[11] *Song of Myself: And Other Poems by Walt Whitman*, Robert Hass, ed. (Berkeley: Counterpoint Press, 2010), 7.

and on and on. Tasks and joys can be a daily spiritual practice, and prayer allows us to savor our living relationship with the Holy and awaken to Divine presence in all. Prayer helps us remember that when we take a single step toward God, God takes a thousand steps toward us. We come to each moment with a wild and excited heart, ready to savor life.

FROM MY SPIRITUAL JOURNAL

> *God is woven into my soul's essence. Together we're the waves and the ocean, the skin and the body, the honeysuckle and its nectar. This sense of presence fills me, asking me for faithfulness and prayer. I sit quietly, without an agenda, and let my soul be absorbed in Divine love. Saturated. My ruby lips soft, receiving this holy kiss.*

PRAYERS AND PRACTICES

1. Engage in "Savoring Prayer." Rest your hands on your lap, and for a few minutes simply savor the energy of delight within. Slow down and be fully present for a few breath cycles. *Breathing in, I am God's delight. Breathing out, I savor this moment.*

2. Engage in journal writing, using the prompt: *In what ways does delight flow in me and in my life?* Feel free to add drawings to your response—colors, shapes, or lines.

3. Remember something that delighted you today and say a prayer of thanks for it.

CLOSING REFLECTIONS

Every day we are alive *in* the gift of creation, *within* Divine love. As our desire for delight and intimacy grows, we become more aware of the boundaries we impose on our heart.

Can you stand in delight, and live with the sense that God delights in the wonder of your being? Do you recognize the amazing life force within you?

Delight is about awakening—recognizing that we're living together in the wondrous gift of creation from the rose to the ocean, from the lions to our fellow human beings, interconnected and interdependent in the oneness of matter and spirit as one life and one living body.

At times, we grow weary with problems and anxieties pressing upon us. We feel stuck and can't access delight or feel a desire to savor. In moments like these, when we have what St. Paul calls "a thorn in my flesh,"[12] bring your thorns—anxieties, stresses, problems—into your love relationship with God.

St. Paul teaches that even when we're weary, rushed, or anxious, we can still allow God to embrace us fully, not to wait till we're some perfect person or image of who we think God wants us to be, or who we think we should be. We

[12] 2 Corinthians 12:7 (NIV).

need to trust that the Spirit will help us handle our thorns, those tender and resistant places, and we can find in them invitations for a faith greater than we can grasp, "our small but necessary offering to any new change or encounter," as Richard Rohr writes.[13]

Thich Nhat Hanh reminds us to water the seeds of joy in ourselves, especially during times of suffering. He writes, "When you are suffering, look deeply at your situation and find the conditions for happiness that are already there, already available. You have eyes that can see, lungs that can breathe, legs that can walk, and lips that can smile."[14]

When we find ourselves at a juncture, we pray, "Our steps are made firm by the Lord, when he delights in our way; though we stumble, we shall not fall headlong, for the Lord holds us by the hand."[15] We are God's children, walking in the mud at times, getting messy, but letting God embrace us and lovingly take delight in us. God is writing us love letters all day long. Every day, we find them in bits and pieces, in glimpses and shadows. *There you are; I see you. I see you.*

---

[13] Rohr, *The Naked Now*, 116.
[14] Thich Nhat Hanh, *The Heart of the Buddha's Teaching: Transforming Suffering into Peace, Joy, and Liberation* (New York: Broadway Books, 1999), 41.
[15] Psalms 37:23-24 (NRSV).

FURTHER JOURNAL EXPLORATION

The Song of Songs is the great love poem in the Hebrew Bible between a young man and a young woman. It can be seen as a metaphor for the mystical love that flows between God and humanity. Read these passages slowly, lingering over the words and allowing your heart to be filled with love and delight, and then reflect on them in your journal.

Imagine yourself saying about the Divine, your Beloved:

> *The voice of my love: listen!*
> *bounding over the mountains*
> *toward me, across the hills.*
>
> *My love is a gazelle, a wild stag.*
> *There he stands on the other side of our wall, gazing*
> *between the stones.*

Imagine God saying to you:

> *And he calls to me:*
> *Hurry, my love, my friend,*
> *and come away!* [16]

---

[16] Chana Bloch and Ariel Bloch, trans., *The Song of Songs* (New York: Modern Library Classics, 2006), 59.

In this next section, can you hear the young man as the voice of the Divine saying to you:

> *And you, my beloved,*
> *how beautiful you are!*
> *Your eyes are doves.*

Can you then be the young woman, and answer:

> *You are beautiful, my king,*
> *and gentle. Wherever we lie*
> *our bed is green.*
> *Our roofbeams are cedar,*
> *our rafters fir.*[17]

- In your journal, reflect on: *How does it feel to hear God calling you "my love, my friend"?* Draw what it feels like—what colors, shapes, lines, and images express this?
- I invite you to read *The Song of Songs* in its entirety and enjoy this poem that celebrates Divine love. I recommend *The Song of Songs*, translated by Chana Bloch and Ariel Bloch. It's lyrical, sensual, and deeply intimate.
- Reflect on this commentary on *The Song of Songs* by twelfth-century French theologian Bernard of Clairvaux: "For the various desires of the soul it is essential that the taste of God's presence be varied too, and that the infused flavor of divine delight

---

[17] Ibid., 53.

should titillate in manifold ways the palate of the soul that seeks him."[18] Pause and reflect upon what is the palate of your soul that seeks God.

---

[18] *Intimacy in Prayer: Wisdom from Bernard of Clairvaux*, compiled by Ephrem Arcement, OSB (Boston: Pauline Books & Media, 2013), 46-47.

THE THIRD INVITATION: EXPANSIVENESS
TRUSTING OUR HEART'S CAPACITY

I want to unfold. Let no place in me hold itself closed,
for where I am closed, I am false. I want to stay clear in your sight.
—RAINER MARIA RILKE[1]

S ince the beginning of our marriage, my husband and
I have created a ritual of asking each other a simple
question: *Where is your home?* It started because we
didn't live near our families and we often felt alone here in
San Francisco. And perhaps it also started because we knew
the love between us was, at the same time, creating a new
home in our hearts. Always, we answer by saying, "*With you,*
in my heart." Sometimes we add the gesture of touching our

---

[1] *Rilke's Book of Hours*, trans. Anita Barrows and Joanna Macy (New York: Riverhead Books, 2005), 59.

hearts while we say these words or touching one another's hearts.

We've shared this ritual many times: when we were tired from work, when we were under pressure due to financial concerns, when we faced infertility and not having children. Each time, in these moments of contraction, we invite ourselves to stay open and expand the capacity of our hearts. After decades of marriage, we still lean into each other with this ritualized willingness to open up to more intimacy so our souls can snuggle up closer.

"In biblical language, *heart* means our whole being, not one or another part of it, rather the center, the source, the taproot of our being,"[2] Brother David Steindl-Rast said in response to a question about how to develop the heart.

Expansiveness is about opening our heart and extending that openhearted stance into the world. Cynthia Bourgeault reminds us that the heart, first and foremost, is an organ of spiritual perception and that by anchoring ourselves *in* the heart, we are able to see from a place of wholeness. Prayer, she reminds us, takes us into the heart, where we experience an inner warmth and our true selves expanding, as we know we are unconditionally loved by God.[3]

Our heart's capacity to love and be loved is beyond what we can grasp. The only limits on the heart are ones we place there. Doubt is not a hindrance. "What is not possible to us

---

[2] Gratefulness.org (gratefulness.org/resource/about-the-heart/).
[3] Cynthia Bourgeault, *The Heart of Centering Prayer: Nondual Christianity in Theory and Practice* (Boulder, Colorado: Shambhala Publications, 2016), 56-58.

by nature, let us ask the Lord to supply by the help of grace," St. Benedict reminded us.[4]

Like Mary Magdalene, the devoted companion of Jesus, we dare to kneel, weeping before the One who loves us, longing to break through the limited ways we see ourselves. When we truly feel our desire for Divine love, we may cry out, *I need you and trust you are there for me.* We say this to God, and to our spouse, our siblings, our friends, and our deepest Self. We depend on the guidance of Spirit to reveal to us, in the depths of our heart, the way to love and be loved. Intimacy is a living, growing experience, not something we force but something we allow and encourage. It may come as bright sunlight or damp mist, in a burst or a soft descent.

Opening and expansion happen through deepening trust, by being gentle with our hearts, and by moving closer to what we love. We follow our nature toward love and become a blooming rose.

1. Finding the Depths of Trust

When we grow in trust, our hearts expand.

> *Blessed is the person who trusts in the Lord,*
> *Whose hope is the Lord,*
> *She is like a tree planted beside the waters*
> *that stretches out its roots to the stream;*

---

[4] Prologue, verse 41 in RB 1980: *The Rule of St. Benedict in English,* eds. Timothy Fry, OSB, et al. (Collegeville, MN: Liturgical Press, 1980).

It fears not the heat when it comes,

its leaves stay green.[5]

This image of "a tree planted beside the waters" reminds us to plant ourselves by the Holy and stretch out our roots to be watered continuously by our trust that God is there. When we are planted by the waters of trust, our leaves will stay green, even in the throes of difficulty, fear, and uncertainty.

I saw this with my mother, who at ninety-two years old faced hip surgery after a bad fall. It was unclear whether the operation would be successful, or even if she would make it. When I spoke to her over the phone the night before surgery, her voice slurring and faint from medications, she kept repeating, "God is with me. God is with us." My mother always held on to this fierce trust, through the birth of ten children, recovery from alcoholism, her daughter's cancer treatment and death, and as a widow for seven years. Over the years, she let the roots of trusting in God's infinite love grow within her.

I could feel her tears in the silence as I wiped away my own. We're asked to have so much trust in the face of the unknown. My mother made it through the surgery but died a month later from heart failure. Her words, "God is with us," stay with me. How many times she said those words, nurturing her trust through a fundamental connection with God and awakening to the truth that she was never separated from God regardless of the circumstances she was

---

[5] Jeremiah 17:7-8 (adapted).

facing. How many times, she said those words to me as I cried over infertility, insomnia, and financial strain.

Trust is at the foundation of all strong and loving relationships, and it allows us to grow into the expansiveness love always offers. With hearts open, we can get closer to God, others, and our deepest self. We are children on the playground, filled with excitement, who stumble, fall, and at times, cry, our flushed cheeks puffed out, our spirit waxing and waning. Yet the Divine keeps picking us up by the hand and telling us, *You're okay. I am with you.* We wipe the dirt off our pant legs, get up, and return to play with renewed joy and zeal, learning again and again to trust.

We have to stay in relationship to the Divine to awaken to the intimacy it offers. We can't stand outside it, just as we can't be married without *being in* the marriage, we can't be a friend without *being in* the friendship, and we can't swim without *being in* the water. Trust depends on participation; we can't trust from the sidelines; we can't trust from the outside looking in. We're called to live *inside* this love relationship.

> "I won't take no for an answer,
>
> God began to say
>
> to me
>
> when He opened His arms each night
>
> wanting us to
>
> dance."
>
> —ST. CATHERINE OF SIENA (FOURTEENTH-CENTURY MYSTIC)[6]

---

[6] Daniel Ladinsky, trans., *Love Poems from God: Twelve Sacred Voices from the East and West* (New York: Penguin Compass, 2002), 186.

Divine love is always offering itself to us. We *experience* the fountain of God's love pouring constantly into our open hearts—passionate, tender, merciful, healing, intimate, steadfast, and renewing—the multitude of ways God is always loving us. This is the wisdom we're invited to awaken to as the petals of Divine love open and expand within us and in our lives. We begin to sense what Mechthild of Magdeburg writes, "Great is the overflow of Divine Love, which is never still but ever ceaselessly and tirelessly pours forth, so that our little vessel is filled to the brim and overflows."[7]

We are called to live inside this love relationship, to experience a dynamic and living relationship with God. We can do this as long as we stay open, and keep surrendering to love, letting love grow in us with God's grace. As the hymn of praise at the close of the Eucharistic Prayer in the Catholic Mass declares: "Through him, and with him, and in him." With these simple words—through, with, in—we glimpse our entire relationship with the Divine.

We recognize we're living in the flow of Divine love, in "this God whom we have named 'Trinity'—the *flow* who flows through everything, without exception, and who has done so since the beginning." [8]

Humbly, slowly, we begin to see that we *are* this Love, for the Spirit is contained in everything—in our hearts and in

---

[7] Carol Lee Flinders, *Enduring Grace: Living Portraits of Seven Women Mystics* (San Francisco: HarperOne, 1993), 69.

[8] Richard Rohr with Mike Morrell, *The Divine Dance: The Trinity and Your Transformation* (London: Society for Promoting Christian Knowledge, 2016), 37.

the sunlight sparkling in each dewdrop atop the tall summer grasses. We trust what's happening beneath the surface in the soil of our souls, the core of our being, even when the rose droops or the petals are jostled in the wind.

FROM MY SPIRITUAL JOURNAL

> Let my heart be open. O Lord of hosts, how blessed is the one who trusts in you! I welcome the sunshine and the rain—all that I am. As my heart bursts open, laughter abounds, sorrow floods me, and tears stream down my cheeks. I hear you call to me, "Trust how much I love you."

PRAYERS AND PRACTICES

1. Using the gift of imagination, pause for a few moments and feel yourself as a plant absorbing the waters of trust. Sense how deep this trust goes, penetrating the soil of your being.

2. In journaling, reflect on your relationship to trust with the prompt: I pray for more trust to_____.

3. Are there any images that speak to you about trust? What does trust look and feel like? Pray with these images and see what they want to reveal to you.

2. Finding a Gentleness of Heart

Intimacy grows through the practice of gentleness—in words, actions, and silence—and this softening helps us to continue finding ways to expand, clear the way, and allow the Divine to bring us closer into the heart of love.

The heart needs gentleness to open, grow, and expand. In her spiritual classic, *Interior Castle*, St. Teresa of Avila writes, "All these interior activities are gentle and peaceful, and to do anything painful brings us harm rather than help. By 'anything painful' I mean anything that we try to force ourselves to do; it would be painful for example, to hold our breath." [9]

Finding ways to cultivate gentleness in our daily lives helps us with this interior growth. I've always found sweeping satisfying. At the end of most days, I like to feel my languid body lean into the wooden broom handle and push the soft bristles across our linoleum kitchen floor. I gather the dust, food crumbs, and strands of hair into neat piles, sweep them into the dustpan, and toss them away. Over the years, I've come to see sweeping as my nightly prayer, a ritual that gently touches my soul, clearing away exterior and interior debris. As I sweep, I feel the Spirit stir in me, and I recognize the need to keep the way within open.

As a girl, living under the same roof as a father who had a volatile temper and four older brothers shouting at the TV during all sorts of football and basketball games, I longed for gentleness. So, when I went to Sunday Mass or whispered prayers under my covers, I needed God to be soft and gentle. I looked for traces of this gentle spirit everywhere and found them in the delicate touch of my

---

[9] Teresa of Avila, *Interior Castle*, 88.

big sister patting me dry after a bubble bath, in the quiet atmosphere of the library on Saturday afternoons, in the softness of Raggedy Ann as I held her each night as I fell asleep. I also found gentleness in stories of Jesus loving the children, weeping over the death of Lazarus, and washing his disciples' feet. Later on, I noticed this gentleness in the young man in his early twenties who later became my husband. He was soft-spoken, kind, and patient, and my heart opened immediately, like the wings of a snowy white egret flying across the infinite love of God, the wings of grace.

In the Christian tradition, St. Paul lists *gentleness* as the sixth fruit of the Spirit: "The fruit of the Spirit is love, joy, peace, patience, kindness, goodness, faithfulness, gentleness, and self-control."[10] Gentleness is also one of nine attributes of a person or community living in accord and alignment with the Spirit. Thomas Keating calls them the nine aspects of the mind of Christ. In *Fruits and Gifts of the Spirit*, he writes, "Gentleness is a participation in God's way of doing things that is at once gentle and firm, sustaining all creation with its enormous diversity, yet without effort."[11]

Some years ago, I coordinated renewal retreats for public school teachers in Northern California and had the privilege of working with spiritual teacher and author Angeles Arrien. During one retreat, Angeles had us gather in the retreat center garden among the fragrant jasmine,

---

[10] Galatians 5:22-23 (NRSV).
[11] Thomas Keating, *Fruits and Gifts of the Spirit* (New York, Lantern Books, 2000), 20.

the sounds of sparrows filling the air. In the sunlight of a beautiful spring afternoon, she directed us to find a place to stand alone but within close proximity to one another, so we still felt like a group.

As we each stood in place, she invited us to feel our feet planted solidly on the ground, and our hearts lifted and open. She invited us to be both strong and soft, and to reflect on these questions: *What do we stand for? What do we stand in?* The teachers expressed their deep desire to stand for their students, and to always stand in integrity and hope.

We learn to stand in gentleness as we expand our hearts and follow our spiritual intuition home to the place of infinite and abiding love. Here we are enfolded in God's tender love, until God becomes "our clothing, who wraps and enfolds us for love, embraces us and shelters us, surrounds us for his love, which is so tender that he may never desert us," as Julian of Norwich writes.[12] In this gentle way, God's grace touches our lives.

We are invited to meet the gentle presence of God, which teaches us how to expand our hearts and treat ourselves and others with kindness and care. Through Divine love, we love one another more, and through this, we grow in our love relationship with God. It's a Divine circle. St. Augustine teaches that when God created us, God created a Capax Dei—a capacity for God. And as James Finley reminds us, "God creates the capacity for loving God, and that's you." The

---

[12] Julian of Norwich, *Showings*, 183.

practice of gentleness allows that capacity to expand within us.

> *The heart opens not by prying it apart like an oyster, but by caressing it. I place my confidence in Your love for me, dear God. A truth my body already holds, and the vessel of my heart contains. We can't stop divine love, swirling and breaking through the self-perpetuating density. Something is becoming lighter. No need to name it. Just let it happen.*

PRAYERS AND PRACTICES

1. Come home to yourself by taking three gentle breaths. Feel the air it flows through your body with each inhale and exhale.

2. As you connect more deeply with your breath, see if you can invite more gentleness into your body and heart. What does this gentleness feel like? Close your eyes for a moment and take it in.

3. Write in your journal using the prompt: *I experience gentleness when* _____. Feel free to add images or drawings.

3. Becoming Willing to Get Closer

At the end of her day, alone in her quiet house in the Southern California desert, my ninety-year-old mother would sit on the white leather chair at her dining room table and in her heart gently ask God, "Did I let you love me today?" The answer was usually *yes.*

My mother unequivocally told me that to love God was to be open to letting God love you. We can choose to get closer to that which we love. Like my late mother, we are propelled by our desire for an intimacy we've never experienced before, a love that touches our deepest longing.

We notice what moves us toward closeness and what pulls us away. A few years ago, I was facilitating a small group of people in a spiritual formation program. The participants were required to engage in a *Daily Awareness* practice to become more aware of how God is active and present in our daily lives. This practice consisted of self-reflection, prayer, and journal writing, and was adapted from a technique described by St. Ignatius of Loyola in the sixteenth century known as the *Examen.*

The question we were asked to explore was *What keeps us open to Divine love and what closes us down?*

I began to keep a *Daily Awareness* journal along with our participants, because I wanted to share in the experience with those I was guiding. After doing this practice for about a month, I began to notice the ways I closed myself off from Divine love by judging myself based on accomplishments and whether I received acknowledgement. If a new guest blog post was accepted or I was invited to give a workshop, I felt good about myself; but when I didn't receive any good news or met rejection, I felt deflated and was attacked by self-criticism.

I continued to pray with this awareness, meeting my need for healing from the deep wounding I carried from my personal history. God's unconditional love was calling me closer, and as I felt more compassion awakening within, I began to notice *how* this unconditional love felt in my heart. It was warm, tender, and spacious. Love is our true nature; God is not interested in our accomplishments, but in our hearts opening into love. Love isn't a concept. It's an experience in the body, and it brings us closer to fullness. We can feel our heart opening and healing taking place.

With prayer, we recognize our constant need for God's tender encouragement. We're like a turtle popping its head in and out of its shell, a soul so tender it needs grace and prayer. We let God lead us back home to the heart of infinite love.

Being loved is an act of freedom, a choice we can make again and again that creates an opening in us and is a prerequisite to caring for others.

FROM MY SPIRITUAL JOURNAL

> Sheltered in Your love, I pray, "Lord keep me in Your Hand." The kitchen window open, warm afternoon sweetness and ripening figs. I am found in the immersion of the porous world. My heart knows the way—and always has. A child's dream is given to a woman, and in the river of her soul, she hears the words: sorrow is loved.

PRAYERS AND PRACTICES

1. Pray with the words of Psalm 139 (NRSV): "You knit me together in my mother's womb." Read the words aloud several times, until you silently sink into them.
2. In your journal, reflect on what keeps you open to love and what closes you from love. Feel free to add drawings and images.
3. Ask God, "Did I let you love me today?"

CLOSING REFLECTIONS

Simply by *seeking* to be closer to God, intimacy with the Divine grows. When we commit to opening our heart and expanding its capacity, love is there. Love is infinite. We are always discovering love—in all our relationships.

During the years my parents were retired and living in Palm Springs, California, I visited them often, and on many occasions my father and I would make pizza together. With precision, like the surgeon he once was, he would carefully measure the flour, olive oil, yeast, and water. I would mix the dough with my hands, place the wet ball in a ceramic bowl, and cover it with a dish towel. My father would set the timer for thirty minutes. Then, we'd sit next to each other at the long kitchen table talking while we waited, the timer going tick-tick-tick. I loved having this time with him, cooking and talking.

I'd wanted to be alone with my father my whole life but having nine brothers and sisters and his preoccupation with his career, it never happened. This time filled a deep hunger in me, and in him. Together in the kitchen, I could hear the low tone of his voice, smell his warm skin, and notice his watery brown eyes concentrating on the meticulous making of pizza.

My father and I opened up more and more to each other during those years. We would talk about marriage, work, and the journey of faith. He was now soft and gentle, and I could easily open up to him. He told me that marriage was like two people rowing a boat together, depending on each other. He shared his struggles with the politics in hospitals, always feeling like an outsider. He also shared his intimate experience of Jesus as a portal to the depth of his heart. In the slow afternoon of the desert heat, making pizza and talking, my father and I became closer and grew in love together. Having this time with him helped heal childhood wounds. It didn't remove them; rather, I grew in the capacity to love and to hold both sorrow and joy. My father and I willingly stepped inside of love, opened to love's presence, and allowed the expansion of our hearts to bring us into a more intimate relationship.

It is the same with God. As we open up to the Divine, giving ourselves more fully, we notice what holds us back, what keeps our hearts hidden. Then with God's gentle hand, we learn to come closer to love. We're called to live in a larger frame, expanding our sense of who we are, who God is, and what life is. Jesus teaches us, *I am the vine, you are the branches, and my Father is the gardener.*[13] Ultimately, we are living in Infinite Love.

We must claim our heritage—to be love, give love, receive love, and live love.

There's not just one way that this manifests. There's only the experience we are having in each moment. We need to honor it, and not get stuck trying to arrange things the way we think they *should* be. When we are living *within* the Spirit, we see that there's more life outside of our assumptions. We take our place next to the prophet Samuel, and simply reply to the call of God, "Here I am." [14]

FURTHER JOURNAL EXPLORATION

Eli encourages the boy Samuel to respond to the call of God by saying, "Speak, Lord, for your servant is listening." This is the call to be open, present, and trusting in the ways the Divine is speaking in our lives.

- Read and pray over this passage from 1 Samuel 3:

    At that time Eli, whose eyesight had begun to grow dim so that he could not see, was lying down in his room; the lamp of God had not

---

[13] John 15: 5 (NIV).
[14] 1 Samuel 3 (NRSV).

yet gone out, and Samuel was lying down in the temple of the LORD, where the ark of God was. Then the LORD called, "Samuel! Samuel!" and he said, "Here I am!" and ran to Eli, and said, "Here I am, for you called me." But he said, "I did not call; lie down again." So he went and lay down. The LORD called again, "Samuel!" Samuel got up and went to Eli, and said, "Here I am, for you called me." But he said, "I did not call, my son; lie down again." Now Samuel did not yet know the LORD, and the word of the LORD had not yet been revealed to him. The LORD called Samuel again, a third time. And he got up and went to Eli, and said, "Here I am, for you called me." Then Eli perceived that the LORD was calling the boy. Therefore Eli said to Samuel, "Go, lie down; and if he calls you, you shall say, 'Speak, LORD, for your servant is listening.'" So Samuel went and lay down in his place.

Now the LORD came and stood there, calling as before, "Samuel! Samuel!" And Samuel said, "Speak, for your servant is listening."

- Pray with this question: In what ways do you hear God calling you at this time in your life? As you pray, can you hear yourself saying, "Here I am"?
- In your journal, write about the ways you felt open

to God's call as you prayed, and the ways you might have felt resistance to it.

• End with a few minutes of silence to integrate your experience.

THE FOURTH INVITATION: ACCEPTANCE

EMBRACING LIFE AND WHO WE ARE

"For it is the unaccepted self that stands in my way—
and will continue to do so as long as it is not accepted."
—THOMAS MERTON [1]

How do we live a relationship with the Sacred that allows God's steadfast love to endure?[2] In my experience, acceptance is the key. The Beloved is longing for us to accept who we are, as we are: recognizing that we were created as *this* leaf, and not *that* leaf. Are we willing to see our gifts and possibilities, as well as our difficult-to-accept limitations? Can we become more willing to accept the ups and downs of life, and accept that the journey of faith includes doubt?

---

[1] *The Intimate Merton: His Life from His Journals*, eds. Patrick Hart and Jonathan Montaldo (San Francisco: HarperSan Francisco, 1999), 130.
[2] Psalms 136 (ESV).

With acceptance of these and other challenges, we meet God's acceptance of us. As James Finley reminds us, "When you have reached the limits of your own abilities to accept difficult aspects of yourself, there may be a point where you begin to feel the beginning of God's infinite acceptance of you as you are."[3] In prayer, quiet and alone, we become naked, undefended before God. Recall the disciple Peter, who on the night of Jesus's arrest denies knowing him three times, and when he does so the third time, "The Lord turned and looked straight at Peter. And Peter went outside and wept bitterly."[4]

Like Peter, we lose our confidence, face our failings, meet our fears, and weep. It happens when we argue within our family, get impatient with a child, become judgmental toward a colleague, or attack ourselves for making a mistake. In moments like these, when met with acceptance by the gentle and compassionate presence of God, we can let our hearts break open. Begging for acceptance, we let Divine love pour into our broken hearts. The more we come out of hiding and allow ourselves to be accepted by God, by ourselves, and by others, the more Divine love can grow in us, and the more intimacy we experience.

Our relationship with God is so much more than we can imagine. Through acceptance, petals unfurl and our relationship with the Divine only deepens. We meet our doubts with understanding and learn to accept others as

---

[3] James Finley, Advent Retreat, Los Angeles, 2019.
[4] Luke 22:60-62 (NIV).

well. Acceptance is an invitation to claim who we are—the person we were born to be, living the life we are meant to live. The more we accept and appreciate ourselves, the more we can live life fully. Merton writes, "Every one of us is shadowed by an illusory person: a false self. This is the man that I want myself to be but who cannot exist, because God does not know anything about him."[5] Acceptance is a gift and a grace that keeps on giving, each time we recognize and accept our true self.

1. Finding Greater Self-Acceptance

We don't have to overcome *all* obstacles, limitations, and doubts before entering an intimate relationship with the Divine. When we see this, we discover a great freedom. We're received by the Divine, and by ourselves, as we are—in our fullness and frailty, our glory and brokenness. Feeling safe enough to look beyond the veil, we dare bring more of ourselves into relationship, becoming honest and relying on love to touch the places within that are crying for care and acceptance. God is devoted to us. We hear the words, *There's no place in you I cannot reach.*

We come with our hearts open, ready, and willing to deepen this Divine relationship through accepting who we are—weaknesses, habits, and all. We trust in the transformative power of love to help us heal and grow. It happens gradually, the way layers of rock form over time. We

---

[5] Merton, *New Seeds*, 34.

encounter our edges—tendencies to judge and the nagging feeling we're not enough. We uncover internal voices and ingrained patterns that pull us away from our essence—*we are made of love and for love.*

I've always struggled with self-acceptance, thinking it only a psychological issue, not a spiritual one. I was intrigued to discover Thomas Merton's journal entries about this. First, on July 2, 1948, he wrote: "There is only one way to peace: be reconciled that of yourself you are what you are." Ten years later, on October 2, 1958, he wrote, "My highest ambition is to be what I already am. That I will never fulfill my obligation to surpass myself unless I first accept myself. When it has been accepted—it is my own steppingstone to what is above me."[6]

The journey of self-acceptance has taken me through the hills and valleys of life, being born into a chaotic, large family with four brothers and five sisters, moving from Philadelphia to Florida to California while my father sought success as a surgeon, my mother struggling with alcoholism. I worked my way through college as a nanny and a housecleaner and married a Jewish man I loved but could not have children with. And throughout the plethora of difficult moments, as well as joyful moments laughing, hugging, and enjoying meals with my husband, friends, and family, I've searched for an authentic connection with the Divine.

With God, we gaze at our stories, at the hidden places

---

[6] Merton, *The Intimate Merton*, 130.

within, and listen to the Spirit with an open heart. Beyond our limited human perspective, in God's way of seeing, we're not alone when we walk life's pathways. Blemishes and scars become beauty marks, and humility gives texture to our lives, revealing the spiritual sweetness of God's embrace.

A few months after my mother's death, I lay in bed one night unable to sleep. Finally, I lit a candle, curled up between the wrinkled sheets, and stared into the flickering light. Tears were streaming down my cheeks. The dream of a different mother, a different life, and a different me were over. The black stamp of night impressed the word *Expired*.

What was over was over. And as I turned on the other side, my back to the candlelight, an invitation from within welled up: *Give it to me. Give it all to me.* The prayer flowed forth from my tongue, and I handed over the wounds I'd carried inside, one by one. *Here, God, is my fantasy of what will never be. Here is my tattered heart. Here is my self-condemnation. Here is my long list of disappointments.*

Take it. Take it. Take it. Ripped jeans. Broken promises. Pages in a girl's diary. All the longing and loss. I was cleaning out the closets of my soul: the worn-out clothes, the shoes that made my feet ache, the self-criticism and feelings of unworthiness and not measuring up. My tears flowed through the house, into the streets, and down to the ocean. As I cleaned out my closeted self, I said, "God, take it all. Into your hands, I entrust my spirit." And I felt the balm of compassion touch inside my raw heart. All the forgiveness and love and mercy I had shared with my mother came flooding back into my heart. I was learning to love beyond what I thought was possible. It was a true experience of deepening intimacy, of growing compassion between me and another. God's love is a healing love.

The more we give ourselves over to love, the more intimacy, connection, and healing we discover. As we learn to practice self-acceptance, we let God show us the way. God completely accepts us, but can we accept ourselves? We allow our relationship with God to become a *real relationship*, not one of approval or to erase the past or one based on feeling we're not enough. We allow ourselves to be fully loved—with all our limitations *and* all our gifts. As Richard Rohr writes, "What I let God see and accept in me also becomes what I can then see and accept in myself. And even more, it becomes that whereby I see everything else."[7] Self-acceptance allows us to receive God's complete love and expand the capacity of our hearts, like the sun shining on a rose so it can grow.

FROM MY SPIRITUAL JOURNAL

> I am longing to accept all of myself—the messiness, the unfolded shirts, my fearful and sometimes foolish thoughts, and my many mistakes. I hear the words of Isaiah, "I have called you my name; you are mine."[8] God is inviting me

---

[7] Rohr, *The Naked Now*, 14.
[8] Isaiah 43:1 (NRSV).

to let go of all preconditions. And to let myself fall, finally, freely into Love's arms.

1. In a stance of self-acceptance, pray with the question: *How can I let myself fall, finally, freely into Love's arms?* Notice what you are being invited to let go, as well as hold on to.

2. In your journal, write about what acceptance would look like in your life, and what it would feel like in your heart. Feel free to add drawings and images.

3. Try hearing God saying to you, "I accept you," when you notice an impatient, critical, or negative voice within. Noticing is a great step in building awareness and moving toward change. Pray for this grace.

2. Meeting Limitations and Doubts

When I was preparing for marriage, I wrote in my journal: *To accept anew each day my partner in marriage as the person entrusted to me by God, to love him as myself.* Entering this union in my mid-twenties, I met my limitations. I found it difficult to relinquish my strong sense of individuality and truly bond with another person. I doubted my capacity to love and be loved. Yet paradoxically, by accepting this doubt and not resisting it, I discovered more faith in myself *and* in my relationship. I remember sharing with a close friend how afraid I was of needing love and needing another person. I didn't want to cling to love, but to see love as a gift rather than a possession.

We can be, in our most intimate relationships, not an image of ourselves, but authentic. We can hear God saying, "Come as you are," calling us to be free of expectations of piety or spiritual confidence. Time and again we will miss the mark and forget, fail, and resist, but "nothing can separate us from God's love," as St. Paul proclaims.[9]

We are invited to be more fully loved—with all our limitations. It isn't easy to stay open when we feel unworthy, or not enough, or when we're attacking ourselves with self-criticism. Yet I've found that in those moments, if I let myself be loved, the foundation of love grows stronger.

During a presentation on St. Teresa of Avila's book, *Interior Castle*, James Finley told this story: "Someone once asked St. Benedict, 'What do you monks do all day in the monastery?' St. Benedict answered, 'We fall down and get up; fall down and get up; fall down and get up.'" Dr. Finley reminded us that, as human beings, our days are filled with *slippage*. "Every time we fall, we are caught by the Love that loves us so."[10] And he added, "It is a love that takes us to itself."

Is falling actually a kind of *embrace with the Divine*? Can

---

[9] Romans 8:31-39 (NRSV).

[10] James Finley, "Teresa of Avila, *Interior Castle*, Center for Action and Contemplation," Santa Fe, New Mexico, online course, June 15, 2019: cac. org/online-ed/interior-castle-course-description/.

acceptance, then, also be about seeing the preciousness of who you are?

It takes courage to allow ourselves to be accepted and loved, just as it takes courage not to be afraid of the waves of doubt that wash over us and disrupt our rhythm and balance? "Doubt is not the opposite of faith; it is an element of faith," wrote twentieth-century theologian Paul Tillich.[11] We learn not to be afraid of it—to remember that we do not have to choose between faith *or* doubt, but rather faith *and* doubt—and even faith, doubt, faith.[12] We can welcome our doubt, and even learn from our dialogue with it. Doubt is what we must walk through as we deepen our faith. By sitting patiently with our doubt, and our limitations, which can be difficult, we discover what's below the surface, a faith that teaches us that something more is happening, and God never rejects us.

As we become more accepting, we tend to be more honest with ourselves, especially during times of uncertainty, knowing we can only rely on grace and that God is our devoted champion. We allow ourselves to be with this Loving Presence without pretense, posturing, or forced conviction. We enter a field out "beyond ideas of wrongdoing and rightdoing,"[13] as the thirteenth-century poet Jelaluddin

---

[11] Paul Tillich, *Systematic Theology*, vol. 2 (Chicago: University of Chicago Press, 1975), 116-117.

[12] Reverend Jacqui Lewis, speaking at the Universal Christ Conference, Albuquerque, New Mexico, March 30, 2019.

[13] *Open Secret: Versions of Rumi*, eds. Coleman Barks and John Moyne (Boulder, CO: Shambhala Publications, 1999), 388.

Rumi writes. There, we let ourselves be completely held in Divine love, trusting that God accepts us as we are.

FROM MY SPIRITUAL JOURNAL

> *I have been hiding—carrying my own list of doubts. It's been raining for weeks. Slow rain, fast rain, drizzling and pouring. I hear the words: "Beloved, where have you hidden?" All is holy—the doubts I carry in my pocket, the atoms of my heart, and shelter on a rainy night. Can I remember that only love has the final say in who I am?*

PRAYERS AND PRACTICES

1. Be willing to meet your doubt, noticing how it feels in your body. Our bodies are speaking to us all the time—if we pay attention.
2. Sit with your doubt and listen to it more deeply through prayer or while writing in your journal. What wisdom is your *doubt* trying to teach you?
3. In prayer, ask God for the grace to hold both doubt and faith.

3. To Dance with God is to Accept Love

I've always loved to dance. As a girl, my older sister and I would turn up the music in our bedroom and swing and shake to the songs of the Monkees. We'd lose ourselves to the lyrics, until we collapsed on our pink shag carpet, laughing hysterically. We danced our way through our mother's alcoholism, our father's moodiness and anger, and our older brothers' tyranny. Later, I danced with girlfriends through the pressures of college to the music of the Talking Heads, and even now, after a long, stressful week at work, my husband and I dance in the living room to the deep pulse of Van Morrison.

There's something about dancing that feels like total acceptance—my body surrendering to the sound, my arms in the air free as a bird, and my loose long hair that has no rules. And when I dance with someone else, we move and respond to each other. In abandoned moments of dancing, I feel as though I'm *accepting* all that life is offering me—the love and the sorrow. As we dance with life, we become our true selves, the person we are in God, and acceptance allows this to happen. To dance with God is to accept love.

Can our acceptance of being loved allow us to open our hearts and offer that profound acceptance to others? One spring, my husband and I were at a busy restaurant in Napa Valley. It was our anniversary, and even though we had a reservation, we had to wait for our table. Sitting on a wooden bench on the patio, I looked at all the people eating and drinking, and my thoughts became judgmental. Fortunately, I noticed my mind's perturbations. I was there to celebrate my anniversary with my husband—to celebrate our love— and I was being unloving toward others. So, I asked myself, how can I be more accepting?

I closed my eyes for a moment and connected to the

Source of love within. As I opened them, I felt an inner shift, and when the maître d' came out to get us, and walked us through the crowded dining room, I found myself saying to each person, silently, as we walked by them, *You are Love. You are Love. You are Love.* Love filled my heart, and I could feel it filling the room! Recognizing love as a shared experience, not a personal possession, gave me new eyes and awakened my heart.

St. Teresa of Avila told her convent sisters that three things are essential in the spiritual life: prayer, self-knowledge, and humility. It felt as though all three were present that night and serve me now as a reminder for reflective action when I notice I've become judgmental. Prayer can be as simple as pausing and taking a few breaths. Self-knowledge can be as basic as recognizing a pattern and, with humility, inviting the Spirit to help us discern right thought and right action.

We're all created from the same love. We are one heart. Recognizing and accepting this love within, I see that love is everyone's true nature. As Richard Rohr said, "The One Life, which we call God, is living itself in you, through you, and as you."[14] You and I and all of us together—there is no separate love.

---

[14] Richard Rohr, from a presentation given at the Universal Christ conference, Albuquerque, New Mexico, March 19, 2019.

My body knows love. For it is love itself—dancing, walking, absorbing the quiet night. The only rule is to give myself permission to say yes to this love. Fully, completely, accepting and embracing who I am. Hair smelling of cinnamon and candlewax. Pouring myself out in love. A wild waterfall rushing through my heart. My nature, my way of being, is my gift to the world.

PRAYERS AND PRACTICES

1. Breathe in acceptance for yourself, letting your heart become full and generous, and breathe out acceptance for others, letting your heart become soft and spacious.

2. Throughout the day, pause and ask yourself: *What would be the most accepting and loving response in this moment: toward myself, toward another, toward a specific situation?*

3. Put on one of your favorite songs and dance with God.

CLOSING REFLECTIONS

A few years ago, I listened to a priest give a homily I've never forgotten. He told us about the tragic loss of one of his siblings when he was much younger. After years of processing his grief, he said to us, "I'm grateful for accepting such hardships in my life, because they have made me more compassionate toward others who may also be suffering. I am more able to offer compassion and empathy because of my experiences." This acceptance and compassion toward ourselves create an opening within that calls us to care for others—in simple and complex circumstances. The awakening of an accepting and compassionate heart for self, others, and the world is needed to hold the brokenness of life with love and hope.

Along with accepting what is difficult, we are also being called to accept what is good. Can we celebrate who we are— our nature, our gifts, our uniqueness? Remember in the creation story when God said, "And it was good." Well, imagine God saying that about you on the day you were born. So often we're trapped in seeing ourselves as everything we are not. But is acceptance asking us to turn that around? As my mother would always say to us, "You are each so different." We're born as a unique thumbprint of creation. Acceptance calls us to embrace our nature, appreciate who we are, and express our gifts. Often, what blocks us from acceptance is comparing ourselves with an idealized other or even an idealized version of ourselves.

Consider this sentiment from the nineteenth-century French saint Thérèse of Lisieux, known as the *Little Flower*. She writes, "If a little flower could speak, it seems to me that it would tell us quite simply all that God has done for it, without hiding any of its gifts. It would not, under the pretext of humility, say that it was not pretty, or that it had not a sweet scent, that the sun had withered its petals, or the storm bruised its stem, if it knew that such were not the case."[15]

We must learn to celebrate ourselves, like the great American poet Walt Whitman declares:

> I celebrate myself, and sing myself.
>
> And what I assume you shall assume,
>
> For every atom belonging to me as good belongs to you.

Once we let ourselves fall into acceptance of ourselves, we can relax and realize that if we could see the miracle of ourselves clearly, our world would change. Responding to life with acceptance requires presence, vigilance, and commitment. When things are going well, acceptance comes easily, but during times of stress or struggle we may face resistance, frustration, disappointment, and overwhelm. When that happens, we can choose acceptance, and we can nurture and strengthen acceptance, with practice.

Practice means creating conditions that allow love to flow from the heart of the Divine into our own heart. It's already flowing; but we need to remember and recognize it to meet and calm the resistance. Acceptance is not about feeling good, but being in an honest relationship with life's ebbs and flows, always remembering the loving voice that cries out: You are precious to Me.

---

[15] *Story of a Soul: The Autobiography of St. Thérèse of Lisieux (the Little Flower)*, trans. John Clark, 3rd ed. (Washington, DC: ICS Publications, 1996), 15

Further Journal Exploration

Pray using Thomas Merton's words that each of us is the presence of love. Journal to hear your own name as love.

- Reflect on these words by Thomas Merton in his classic book, *New Seeds of Contemplation*: "To say that I am made in the image of God is to say that love is the reason for my existence, for God is love. Love is my true identity. Selflessness is my true self. Love is my true character. Love is my name."[16]
- Write the ways God is calling you to see that love is *your* true identity. Try drawing with shapes and colors what this looks like to you.
- Write the ways God is inviting you to see *others* as the presence of love.
- Write what a radical recognition of love might look like in your life and how it would feel in your heart. It will become your manifesto of love!

---

[16] Merton, *New Seeds*, 60.

THE FIFTH INVITATION:
VULNERABILITY
BECOMING OPEN-HEARTED

"The work of the Spirit is to keep you vulnerable
to life and love itself."[1]
— RICHARD ROHR, OFM

A few years ago, on a painting retreat, I shared a large studio with four other artists. I usually prefer working alone, so being in a shared space made me feel exposed. Along with the sound of brushes on canvas, I heard my own self-doubts and judgments. How could I let others see my process, my imperfect and flawed work? I wanted to hide, yet another part of me wanted to stay, recognizing the healing power of witnessing and being seen.

As I looked at the other painters, I sensed that they, too, were vulnerable, and I was reminded of the reverence I felt

---

[1] Richard Rohr, cac.org/vulnerability-2016-09-27/.

at Sunday Mass, walking up the aisle with others to receive communion. Each person stood in front of the priest and congregation exposing his or her longing to connect more deeply with God. Filled with a burning desire to create, connect, and share the power of creativity with others, I knew I wanted to stay put and be part of the group.

I had grown up guarding my heart from what was around me—my alcoholic mother, moody father, and aggressive older siblings. Although I longed to be seen by those around me, I was gripped by insecurity. Slowly, over years, through loving friendships and my marriage, through art classes and sharing my paintings, through retreats and finding a faith community, I let go of my fears, was able to give them to God for healing, and my interior darkness found light.

The word *vulnerable* comes from the Latin *vulnerare*, "to wound," and was later used to mean "defenseless." Vulnerability suggests risk and uncertainty. Yet, as priest and theologian Henri Nouwen wrote, "Nobody escapes being wounded. We are all wounded people, whether physically, emotionally, mentally, or spiritually. When our wounds cease to be a source of shame and become a source of healing, we have become wounded healers. Jesus is God's wounded healer."[2]

Vulnerability is an experience we take part in all the time—as we sit in a doctor's office, lose a job, get married, watch our parents age and become frail. To be human is to be vulnerable. Our days and years are marked by one

---

[2] Henri Nouwen Society, henrinouwen.org/meditation/the-wounded-healer/.

vulnerable moment after another. It's our common ground. I feel it in the sobbing of a friend over a parent's sudden death, in my husband reading me a poem he wrote, in my sister going on dates again, longing to fall in love. The more we live in our heart, the more vulnerable we become.

That day in the studio, we were each facing the unknown, together—searching for a line, a shape, a color. I wanted to stand inside, where risk and growth happen. I felt in the ochre paint on my brush the urge in my heart that didn't want to hold back, just as when I'd received communion. I pressed my brush on the canvas, raw and vulnerable, and continued.

Can we welcome vulnerability, trusting that it leads to a deepening of love and intimacy? Being vulnerable, letting our guard down and being held in the vast container of love when we're strong and when we're weak takes courage. Embodying vulnerability is a necessary step for living a life of intimacy and love. We can develop an inner stance toward vulnerability by taking more risks in love, allowing ourselves to be truly seen, and being ourselves more—with God and with others.

1. Taking Risks in Love

When I spent time with my mother during the last years of her life, we'd sit at her black Formica dining table—just the two of us—talking, catching up, sharing memories. When I noticed strong feelings welling up inside me from years of her being absent, I expressed them. I cried freely, releasing the heaviness stored in the pit of my stomach. "It hurt so much," I told her. She would receive my tears and cry her own, telling me how much she missed being my mother during her time of addiction.

Our relationship became more inclusive of sorrow and joy, tears and laughter, talking and silence. By being more vulnerable with each other, our relationship became more dynamic, capable of holding a wide range of emotions. The more we risk in relationships, the more generous and forgiving we become, and the result is intimacy. When we let the limitless love of God flow into our lives, we find the courage to risk sharing deeply the most vulnerable parts of ourselves.

During the first few years of my marriage, I would awaken in the middle of the night and listen in the dark to my husband's breathing, the ephemeral weight of his exhalation filling my ears. Here we were, breathing next to one another in bed, joining our lives together. How vulnerable I felt. *God, let me love*, I would pray. I was giving myself to another, who was giving himself to me, and the longings of our hearts were transforming us both. My heart beat wildly inside my small frame. This love was so big, at times I could hardly breathe. Could I bear exposing myself like a night heron in the moonlight?

We dare to step inside our hearts, into a love that grows from vulnerability, into a love that can meet the tender places within—our wounds, our insecurities, and our hopes for intimacy and connection. I discovered that the more I was able to align myself with Divine love, the more vulnerable I felt safe to feel.

We are invited to give ourselves to the Divine, allowing the love in our hearts to flow like a rushing river. *I am nothing without you.* We dare love God with that much surrender. Our hearts break open, and we find ourselves *inside* Divine love, vulnerable, meeting its healing power. God's love grounds us and holds us steady, so our hearts can lift from Spirit's grace.

Through prayer, meditation, and devotion, we can become rooted in Divine love, safe in the home of the heart, dwelling in union with love's presence. We become more willing to share our feelings, expose our fragility, and risk stumbling and falling. We let ourselves become like the woman in the Gospel of Luke[3] who had been hemorrhaging for twelve years. She was willing to risk and reach out with her deepest desire for love, wholeness, and healing and had the courage to touch the fringe of Jesus's cloak. We, too, must risk and reach out, and have our own deeply personal relationship with the Divine. We need to have the courage to call God "friend, beloved, confidant, healer," to let this mysterious relationship unfold in all its fullness.

As St. Teresa of Avila, teaches us, God is our constant companion. She writes, "The will shows the soul how this true Lover never leaves it, but goes with it everywhere and gives it life and being. Then the understanding comes

---

[3] Luke 8:43-48 (NRSV).

forward and makes the soul realize that for however many years it may live, it can never hope to have a better friend."[4]

We can extend our capacity to live a more intimate life by being more vulnerable and taking risks in our many different relationships. One day at work, a relatively new fifth-grade teacher rushed into the library, running late to pick up his students. Many of his students read below grade level, and others had weak math skills. As they were lining up to leave, he blurted out, "Maybe some of the kids could work with a volunteer during library and not waste their time in here."

After he left, I felt uneasy, as though my efforts were reduced to unimportant and nonessential. I decided to take a risk and went to his classroom during our lunch break to express my feelings, and he acknowledged them. He apologized for "his poor choice of words," while I acknowledged his concern for his students' low skill level. At the end of our talk, we shook hands as a gesture of reconciliation. We'd both chosen not to get defensive, but to be honest and vulnerable and clear the air between us.

Taking risks and being vulnerable can bring depth and sincerity to relationships. To be vulnerable is to let love get bigger so it can fill the sanctuary of our hearts with the gifts of compassion, trust, and faith. We learn to trust the Spirit at work: in the emptying out and giving of love, as well as in the constant infilling and generosity of love.

God is always whispering in our hearts, *I'm here.* We need

---

[4] Teresa of Avila, *Interior Castle*, 48-49.

God's tender love to hold all the brokenness, to be the Source of our vulnerability. We learn to follow the way of the blind beggar Bartimaeus sitting on the side of the road crying out, "Son of David, have mercy on me!" and hearing Jesus say, "Your faith has healed you."[5] This is faith in love, faith in being vulnerable to love.

Our love relationship with the Divine, with each other, and with all of life requires us to take risks and let our hearts plunge into unfathomable depths. Vulnerable, we feel ourselves losing our edge and being absorbed into a greater wholeness. We remove our armor and trust our vulnerability, ready to be both wounded and fulfilled. Vulnerability, a kind of surrendering, is essential to spiritual growth. Brené Brown reminds us, "If we want greater clarity in our purpose or deeper and more meaningful spiritual lives, vulnerability is the path."[6]

Accepting vulnerability, we recognize love as an interconnected, interdependent experience. Without God, without each other, and without the beauty of the mountains, how could love unfold?

FROM MY SPIRITUAL JOURNAL

> I am living inside of love, roaming in the open and fragrant fields. We cannot possess love, but only be absorbed by it and in it. By its very nature, love is vulnerable, broken, and

---

[5] Luke 18:38-42 (NIV).
[6] Brené Brown, *Daring Greatly: How the Courage to Be Vulnerable Transforms the Way We Live, Love, Parent, and Lead* (New York: Avery/Penguin Random House, 2012), 34.

shared. I ask myself: "What's it like to feel empty?" I only know that in the whispering wind, I hear I am a divine desire, a longing for God. And I trust I will be satisfied.

PRAYERS AND PRACTICES

1. Pause and ask yourself: *How am I feeling?* Sit with the question a few minutes; really tune into your body, and let the true answer emerge. If you're feeling sad, receive it. If you're happy, receive it. If you're tired, receive it.
2. Invite God into this moment with you. Be willing to bring all of you into this sacred moment. Be willing to be honest.
3. Write a dialogue between you and God about how you're feeling. Start the dialogue by expressing your feelings. *Dear One, I'm feeling angry right now,* or *happy right now.*

2. Letting Ourselves Be Seen

As we reveal ourselves, intimacy grows. We're invited to bring more of ourselves—our brokenness, flaws, beauty, and desires—into this Divine love relationship, so we can meet unfolding joy, sorrow, desolation, consolation, doubt, delight, and surprise fully. We experience that in God's gentle presence, we are more able to be present to ourselves.

As we expose our hearts, we feel the need for Divine love

even more acutely. We ache for it, long for it, and depend on it. Being vulnerable with the Divine is the ultimate vulnerability. We let ourselves be seen and loved *as we are*, defenseless and with humility. "Humility is not false modesty, but the true realization that without God we are nothing," states James Finley.[7] We don't need to judge the highs and lows of the journey, not the times of joy or the times of darkness. All of it can lead to a deeper trust in God. This long-lasting relationship requires daily commitment. We learn to live inside this love, which is always offering itself to us in unexpected and mysterious ways.

In the courtyard of St. Mary's Elementary School, in Miami, Florida, I looked up at Mary, the Holy Mother, eight feet tall, made of alabaster. The smooth white statue watched over all of us and became my friend. Running up to her every morning for six years, I could feel her strength and gentleness, her compassionate eyes always looking down upon me. In front of her, I felt seen in a way that was never true in my family, where my mother often called me by my sister's name, and I was referred to as "number eight" (of ten children).

Alabaster Mary was larger and stronger than any woman I knew. As I stood in her presence, I felt held in grace. Every day with my palms touching in front of my heart, I would say, "Hail Mary, full of grace." I loved saying those words and wondered, "Could I be full of grace, too?"

---

[7] Offered by James Finley in a talk for the Living School Symposium, August 5-8, 2018.

I liked telling Mary the little things I did, like how my sister and I would whisper to each other from our twin beds after the lights were shut until we fell asleep. I'd tell her about the big things too, that my mother was drinking and how scared it made me feel. Every day when I visited Mother Mary, she looked at me with a mother's love. I could step into her eyes and rest my head upon her heart.

Spiritual ancestors—saints, mystics, and teachers—help us trust what we hold in our hearts. Without being conscious of it, Mary became my spiritual mother and held my vulnerability. Our hearts long for recognition and companionship as we step into the unknown depths of our hearts.

The intimacy of being seen is both disarming and comforting, encouraging us toward life and love. In my work as a librarian and a spiritual director, I've come to see that vulnerability is inherent to the human experience.

Every week, an eight-year-old with thick brown braids comes into our school library for something to read. She's a beginning reader and desperately wants to read more. Over the years, I've become sensitive to how vulnerable children feel about being able to read. I watch her searching the shelves, picking up *Charlotte's Web* or *Charlie and the Chocolate Factory*, holding it for a while, then putting it down. I give her time, then show her picture books with words she can read. "You may like one of these," I say, flipping through the pages. She always chooses my suggestions and hugs the book close to her chest as she leaves with her class. To allow our needs and imperfections to be seen by others and by

God is the essence of vulnerability. Each expression of vulnerability is a call to be seen, to let the petals of our heart be revealed.

One midweek afternoon, I was feeling overwhelmed by deadlines, demands, and internal pressures. I sat alone in my dining room, the sun peering through the cream linen curtains. As I watched the shadows move across the table, I allowed myself to be with my feelings, and I sensed my heart heavy, as though filled with sand. I picked up the phone and called my younger sister.

"It's all too much," I cried, needing reassurance. "It's okay, just cry," she said. As I let myself be heard, I could feel my sister holding me with her kindness and presence. She stayed on the line as long as I needed, until the room softened with the dusk. "Thanks," I said. "Call me later, if you need to," she said as we hung up.

Sometimes, the people we love remind us what it means to be intimate with God, to allow ourselves to lean into our needs and feel cradled and cared for in our vulnerability. We are called to be witnessed and received as we are. No part of us excluded.

FROM MY SPIRITUAL JOURNAL

Remove your sandals, you are standing on Holy Ground. Don't run away or hide. Be yourself, sweet one. Be, Colette. Love is about giving yourself away. Come in through your belly. I'm ready to let your waters wash over me. Love is

*pouring into me; feels so good not to control it. I'm ready,
God, to let the rivers of love wash over me.*

PRAYERS AND PRACTICES

1. Permission can be a spiritual practice inviting you
   to reveal more and more of yourself. In the presence
   of the Holy, pray with the question: Where in my
   life am I being called to say *yes*; where am I being
   called to say *no*? Don't rush the answer; sit with the
   question as long as you need and see what arises.

2. Write in your journal whatever comes up for you—
   as simple or complex as that may be.

3. Discern what actions you might take to manifest
   your *yes*.

3. Being More Ourselves with God and Others

One morning under the glow of golden autumn light, I
drove along Fulton Street on my way to St. Ignatius Church
in San Francisco. I'd been up since the middle of the night,
unable to rest, unable to let go, which often happens when
I worry about money or my job, or when my heart is aching
from losing someone I love. I felt tired and vulnerable, holding it all in so I wouldn't spiral into despair. I made my way
to early Mass, a lifeboat of hope for me.

Although it's a grand church with high vaulted ceilings,
large oil paintings, and royal red carpet down the center

aisle, the morning Mass is always held at one of the side alcoves. Here, at a simple wooden altar in the womb of the cavernous church, a group of about twenty regulars who attend weekly Mass were gathered. We prayed quietly, the silence generous and palpable, honoring this time of solitude within community, being alone with others. The light diffuses through the filter of the stain glass windows, we were removed from the pressures of time. This was my soul time, cradled in the lullaby of the Divine.

I sat in the wooden pew wrapped in my gray scarf, taking in the sweet fragrance lingering in the air—cedar, sandalwood, and frankincense. Here I was able to be myself in all my vulnerability, feeling safe in this sacred space, in this community of silence. I closed my eyes and sank deeply within, and when I felt it was right, I opened my eyes, smiled, and connected with others. This was the permission we gave ourselves and each other, the same faces dotting the pews year after year. Then morning Mass began, slipping through the silence like a button through a buttonhole. I was a pilgrim of the morning, and the stormy fears of the night had found a place to rest, a shelter, a home.

Being vulnerable is key to love growing and deepening, as it has over the years with my relationship with God, with my husband, and with friends, relatives, and colleagues. Each step of the way, I've learned to trust my heart and others' hearts, and to share who I really am with the fears and risks of being vulnerable. Surprisingly, my job as a librarian has helped me grow in my ability to be truly seen in front of others. In the presence of children, reading stories filled with talking animals, magical moments, and children overcoming their fears, I've found an authenticity in myself, a way of being expressive and relaxed.

At times, I'll be reading a story aloud, only to look up and see twenty-two pairs of eyes enraptured in the magic of the tale, hanging on to the sounds of my voice. In those moments, I feel the presence of Spirit and realize it's my willingness to be vulnerable—sensitive and unrehearsed—that allows this exchange to be sincere and meaningful for all.

God wants only that we be the person we were created to be—not some*thing* or some*one* else. In his essay "Things in Their Identity," Thomas Merton writes, "We are at liberty to be real, or to be unreal. We may be true or false, the choice is ours."[8] We can live our lives wearing a mask or we can remove it and come boldly forward. This is the unfolding of the rosebud, revealing her inner secrets, understanding her need for boundaries and safety while opening to the fullness of her desire and expression. My experience entering love in all its varieties has shown me ways that vulnerability can be a strength. Vulnerability encourages intimacy.

Over the course of our long marriage, my husband and I have been becoming more and more ourselves and catching glimpses of each other. We continue to discover the tender places where our hearts are fragile, and have been willing

---

[8] Merton, *New Seeds*, 32-33.

to show each other these places, to touch them, and not to hide. In this way, we're continually learning the ways of love—by loving. Relationships are the school for love.

I look at a photo that captures a moment in our early thirties—a photo of us sitting on a stone wall in Golden Gate Park snapped by his parents. Our faces are turned toward each other, our chins and noses lined up, and we're smiling with ease and generosity. I am saying *yes* to his love with unsullied assurance, my eyes taking him in like a magnet. His eyes twinkle, too, as he looks at me, sunlight streaking across the bridge of his nose, the glow of heaven surrounding us.

In another photo, a decade later, my husband's long arm is draped across my back and around my shoulder. We look like limbs of the same tree. I can still smell the hint of dark chocolate on his lips. In this one, we're each wearing a brown coat, mine wool, his leather, a sign of solidarity.

And in a more recent selfie taken in Hawaii, our faces are more rugged, creases across his forehead, salt-and-pepper hair framing my face, but still in the spontaneity of love. He's shirtless, grinning, smelling of the ocean. My lips are pressed to his cheek so hard that my nose flattens. Only half my face is visible, one round eye as deep as a whale's is looking ahead. Our skin sticky after a day at the beach, we're present with our authentic selves and full of love— love of life, love of nature, love for each other knitted into a moment of time and into the vastness of the universe.

This moment, that moment, glimpses of becoming ourselves and falling more and more in love. It's the same with the Divine. Over the years, I catch glimpses of God, and as I become more myself, we fall more and more in love—its vastness and its particularities. We are all invited to bring the fragments of our hearts into the Divine's infinite, generous love. We are invited to participate, to let the Spirit teach us to love, one vulnerable moment to the next, becoming more and more of ourselves and becoming more and more of Divine love along the way.

FROM MY SPIRITUAL JOURNAL

At first, I wanted you to look something like I had imagined. But as the lines of time bent into your skin, rougher now, I see you as you are—eternal, mountainous, more than I ever could have imagined. Oh, blessed be that which is true to itself. Time formed and time broken. Kiss me. The sound that has no name is, I know now, your voice.

PRAYERS AND PRACTICES

1. Take a few breaths and let yourself arrive in this present moment. Relax with each inhalation and exhalation. Invite yourself to feel a sense of ease.

2. Ask the Divine in prayer: *May the door of vulnerability be open in my heart.*

3. In your journal, write and draw using the prompt:

I can be more vulnerable with God and others by_____.

CLOSING REFLECTIONS

In the twelfth century, Hildegard of Bingen permitted her nuns to let their hair down for liturgical celebrations. They were encouraged to go before God uncovered, exposed, and full of desire. We can also give ourselves permission to come before the Holy with our hair down, with only love burning in our hearts. Meeting God in the intimacy of our vulnerable hearts, we let ourselves be loved as we are. *True love is not a belief system. It's an experience*, one that only happens with vulnerability.

It's only with vulnerability that love can stay alive, and the promise of love can fulfill itself in joy and sorrow. When we encounter our tendency to drift away, we remember the need to keep turning toward Divine love. In times of doubt and uncertainty, we're called to trust, just like the disciples who, after being at sea all night and catching nothing, listen to Jesus when he tells them, "Cast the net on the right-hand of the boat and you will find a catch." So, they did, and then they were not able to haul in a great number of fish.[9] We can hear God inviting us to let go and trust, that we're not alone, to know that we're in a unitive relationship with Divine love.

As in our relationship with a beloved, we hear the calling

---

[9] John 21:6 (NRSV).

to become more vulnerable so our relationship can deepen and become more committed. Again and again, we find ourselves pulling back, saying, "I can't say this; I can't feel that." But we persevere in seeking the intimacy we know God is offering us, always.

As a result of this resolve, we begin to catch glimpses of the Divine in the mirror throughout the day. We smile, and God smiles back, seeing us, our efforts and our dreams. We meet and trust this abounding, steadfast love. Without vulnerability, intimacy is never complete. To have our own deeply personal relationship with the Divine, we must share the deepest, hidden parts of ourselves, and filled with sweetness and longing, open ourselves to intimacy.

FURTHER JOURNAL EXPLORATION

We pray and engage in journaling with the writing of St. Catherine of Siena on love and vulnerability. Slowly read this poem she wrote in the fourteenth century:

> *Vulnerable we are, like an infant.*
> *We need each other's care*
> *or we will*
> *suffer.*[10]

- Read the poem again, aloud, and notice which word

---

[10] Ladinsky, trans., *Love Poems*, 185.

or phrase resonates for you. Spend time in prayer and let the word or phrase enter your heart, and discover what it means to you.

- In your journal, reflect upon what vulnerability means to you at this time in your life.

THE SIXTH INVITATION:
MYSTERY

DWELLING IN THE MYSTERY OF LOVE

"The most beautiful thing we can experience is the mysterious."
— ALBERT EINSTEIN[1]

I fell in love with the young man who would become my husband in a split second at a café in Montréal. It was a cold winter's night and we were both waiting in line at the coat check. I asked him, a stranger, if he knew a place where my friends and I might go dancing. As our eyes met, I was touched by mystery. In that moment of grace, we stepped into each other's hearts. Now, three decades later, I meet him daily as we wake together, and I greet him with each new day. I loved my husband from the moment I met him, and we have been falling in love again and again, one moment to the next, ever since. This is the mystery of love.

---

[1] Albert Einstein, *Living Philosophies* (New York: AMS Press, 1931).

Mystery comes from the Latin *mysterium*, which means "a secret thing." It is profound and inexplicable, something we cannot fully understand, but can touch and know in the depth of our hearts. "There's Divine gravity pulling us within to where the Beloved is in us," said Camaldolese monk Michael Fish during a retreat on contemplative living. Here in this sacred place within, the Beloved is inviting us to look at all of life with Divine eyes, where the ancient is always new, and the familiar is always strange.[2]

How do we learn to dwell in this mystery—this secret thing we can't fully understand? How can we live a life of love that has space for the unknown?

Love humbles us; it's tender, magnificent, and ungraspable. All we can do, with faithfulness, is give ourselves over to this sacred source of life. As we surrender, love guides us into who we truly are, which is love. This is the journey of the rose, day and night, held inside a depth of love that is immeasurable and limitless. It takes humility and grace to sustain the gaze and dwell within this mystery.

We enter into communion with mystery in three distinct ways: seeing our relationship with the Divine as dynamic; following our desire to discover love; and allowing ourselves to trust in this mystery, to be in the unknown where intimacy deepens with faith.

In the depths of our heart, love's mystery unfolds, always giving itself to us, and we in turn always give ourselves to

---

[2] Michael Fish, Retreat on "The Camino-Life's Journey," San Rafael, California, July 13, 2109.

love. We are in relationship to the mystery, and the mystery is in relationship to us. Inside this union, sharing in God's life and creation, we belong. We lean back on the warm hood of our car on a clear night and let the star-studded sky absorb us, and for a moment, we become the deep darkness and the shimmering light, touching boundlessness, "encircled by the arms of the mystery of God," as Hildegard of Bingen reminds us.[3]

1. *Seeing our relationship with the Divine as dynamic*

Our relationship with the Divine is dynamic, alive. It grows as we grow and expands as our appreciation of God's mystery deepens. Our relationship with the Divine is in our relationship with creation, nature, and all that is vibrant and sacred, fertile and in flux, vigorous and purposeful. The holy mystery of creation and spirit is alive in every moment. We only need to notice it.

Hiking along a bluff in Northern California last summer, the Pacific Ocean stretched on one side and the dense spruce and pine forest on the other, I felt myself walking in the generosity of God. All I was seeing—pine needles, the eyes of an eagle, sunlight glistening on the ocean, my husband walking in front of me, my feet on the moist earth—everything was a footprint of the Divine, the Mystery

---

[3] Avis Clendenen, *Experiencing Hildegard: Jungian Perspectives* (Asheville, NC: Chiron Publications, 2012), 9.

revealing itself. As we continued walking, I felt the wind as my breath: one step, one breath.

We are living in the *Divine Milieu*, as Teilhard de Chardin proclaimed. According to theologian Ursula King, Teilhard was trying to capture the meaning of two different experiences—the environment and atmosphere that surround us and a center point where all realities converge. King states, "The divine presence in the world is this mysterious milieu radiating throughout all the levels of the universe, through matter, life, and human experience."[4] Spirit and matter are inseparable. Within every speck of matter, every rock and teardrop, every nuance and eruption is the impulse and dynamism of Divine love.

Spirit is inherent, not something added on. Richard Rohr teaches, "Matter and spirit reveal and manifest each other."[5] Our journey is to discover how to enter more fully into this dynamic flow, let it transform and heal us, and teach us how to perceive life from a place of wholeness. How this happens is unique in each of our lives.

Once during fall, I was in Washington State, at a small gathering with fourteen other women exploring the theme of creativity and spirituality. We engaged in the expressive arts, dance, song, art, and writing poetry as ways to awaken the Creative Spirit to which we're all connected, the Divine

---

[4] Ursula King, *Pierre Teilhard De Chardin: Modern Spiritual Masters Series* (Maryknoll, New York: Orbis Books, 1999), 57.
[5] Richard Rohr, *The Universal Christ: How a Forgotten Reality Can Change Everything We See, Hope For, and Believe* (New York: Convergent Books, 2019), 239.

that is expressed uniquely through each of us. Halfway through the week, we made plaster masks of each other, and when my partner lifted the white, still damp, mask off my face, my first comments were, "My nostrils look so large," "Why are my cheeks sunken in?" and "I don't have any lips."

In the midst of creative expression, the voice of judgment attacked me, allowing old wounds to resurface—my father's harsh voice, my older siblings' competitive badgering, the loneliness from my mother's absence. Over the years, my self-esteem fell so low I never spoke up in college, and I lost faith in myself. Through prayer, therapy, self-compassion, and the gifts of love, I've been healing, but time and time again, self-criticism stings me like a hungry mosquito, telling me all that I'm not and will never be.

That night, after seeing the plaster cast of my face and reacting as I did, I was awake at 4:00 a.m. listening to the raindrops tapping on the thin window. The sound became a companion in the dark as I lay on my back, the covers pulled up to my chin, and I pressed my hands gently over my heart. I was meeting my wounded places with a tenderness that felt soft and caring, pure and effusive, steady and constant. They were asking for my trust.

My heart began to tremble as it opened, and love began to seep in. It was geologic movement in my body, a rising up and breaking through of the mystery of Divine love. Love was awakening in me: deepening and widening; swirling and penetrating; reaching my entire being through the channel of my heart. I was alive in God's love. My heart knew it and was leading the way, transforming and transcending the ache of self-criticism and judgment.

I stayed in bed until dawn, letting love do love's work as the rain continued to softly tap against the windowpane. All I could hear between the drops and my tears was, *You don't need to understand it. Let Love Heal You.* Love is a mystery and a healer.

To allow the Divine's dynamic love to have its way with us is "to work together with God in the creation of our life," as Merton exclaims.[6] Love pours into us so it can pour out of us. It is circular, like giving and receiving a hug, like the rhythm of dawn and dusk.

At rest or in prayer, or when walking, if we take a moment away from the frenetic blur of our usual busyness, we can feel the mystery touch us—in our heart, in our body, in our breath. The secret reveals itself in the rustling of leaves during an evening walk; when we inhale the sweet, familiar scent of our beloved; or when our breath becomes a whisper in the ear of the Divine. We let ourselves be known beyond any understanding we've ever had of ourselves, and trust that "the only One who can teach me to find God is God, Himself, alone," as Merton wrote.[7] Our life is a conversation with God. We shake with tears and laughter, at one with the Divine mystery—being and becoming alive again in a visceral, organic, creative dance.

---

[6] Merton, *New Seeds*, 32.
[7] Ibid., 6.

> *The mystery I'm looking for is inside me. I tell my mind,*
> *Hush, you don't need to know everything. I listen for the*
> *silence between the notes. Some truths are only revealed*
> *in a split second. I feel a shadow behind me, my feet on a*
> *definite edge. I repeat the words of Rumi, "Don't move the*
> *way fear makes you move."*[8]

PRAYERS AND PRACTICES

1. The opening lines of the Bible introduce us to the *Divine Breath*, the dynamic basis of all being and all life. Contemplatively read from Genesis 1:1-2, "and the Breath of God was moving over the face of the waters." Read this phrase slowly, several times, allowing the words to come alive.

2. God's breath is your breath, and your breath is God's breath. Take two or three deep breaths and feel the way your breath can connect you with the dynamic flow of the Divine presence, here and now.

3. Allow a prayer to arise from this awareness.

2. Seeking and discovering the mystery of love

Mystery invites us to seek and then discover what might be hidden behind a curtain. It asks us to look closely and

---

[8] *Rumi: Selected Poems*, trans. Coleman Barks et al. (New York: Penguin, 2004), 278.

expansively at all we encounter and re-encounter—the luminous moon, the sparkle in a child's eyes, the roses blooming, the moments of prayer. People often seek spiritual direction to discover more of their connection, experience, and relationship with the Divine *and* with their own lives and loved ones. They come with a yearning to discover what lies beyond all they know, and this often leads to a deep respect for the unknown, the ultimate Mystery. They are seeking a sense of love, belonging, and connection. They are seeking to discover the presence and action of God in their hearts and in their lives.

God is also seeking us, as Rabbi Abraham Joshua Heschel states in his book *God in Search of Man*. From the beginning, he writes, "the Lord called: *Where art thou* (Genesis 3:9). It is a call that goes out again and again. It is a still small echo of a still small voice, not uttered in words, not conveyed in categories of the mind, but ineffable and mysterious, as ineffable and mysterious as the glory that fills the whole world. It is wrapped in silence; concealed and subdued, yet it is as if all things were the echo of the question: *Where art thou?*"[9]

At nineteen, my father experienced this mutual searching within his soul in a moment that redefined his life. He was searching for God, and God was searching for him. One cold night in Philadelphia, with his fingers numb and slipped into his pockets, he was walking home on his usual route, past the Catholic Church. He was a night worker, a

---

[9] Abraham Joshua Heschel, *God in Search of Man* (New York: Farrar, Straus and Giroux, 1955), 136-137.

washroom attendant at an upscale hotel and bar. He saw the door to the church open and turned toward the light. He walked in to warm himself, or perhaps because something was pulling him. The pews were filled with other night workers: bakers, janitors, security guards, and nurses. The smell of fried donuts, harsh ammonia, sweat, grease, and dreams lingered in the air, mixing with frankincense and candle wax.

My father followed his heart into the church, and never looked back. He converted to Catholicism. God had caught him, and the next sixty years he spent tracing this experience. His heart forever whispering in the wind, roaring in the desert. God works in mysterious ways.

We want to know life and God and all the reasons for existence, suffering, and love, but we can't. So, more and more, we learn to give it all to God—all the unknowing we consistently touch. We're called to become more at home in darkness, but it is a darkness illumined by faith and discovered in the heart, for "the heart that breaks open can contain the whole universe,"[10] exclaims eco-activist and writer Joanna Macy. We're like astronauts, learning to float in zero gravity, in a state of freefall, the absolute mystery and beauty of darkness.

In the depth and secret of our hearts, we are always encountering the mystery. As a girl, I loved to swing in the backyard of our Florida home. We had a swing set with wooden seats, long chains, and plenty of room to soar.

[10] Joanna Macy, spoken in a workshop.

Whenever I could, between homework and chores, I'd run outside and swing. With each thrust of my legs taking me higher and higher, I felt the breeze caressing me. I wanted to touch the sky, to feel God's breath on my skin, to be smothered by the sun and the air until I was giddy. Once airborne, I no longer felt the weight of constant chores, or my unhappy family. Swinging and swinging, the heaviness was lifted from me and I was carried by God's communion.

We encounter the mystery of Divine love by entering into the heart's desire for union—to swing, to search, to feel the edges and shadows. Emerging from this, we feel deeply our love for all those in our lives: our spouses, families, friends, colleagues, and even strangers whose names we may never know. In hundreds of moments like these, the infinite light falls across our faces and wraps around our hearts. "St. Teresa of Avila likened her experience of the divine union to sunlight pouring through two windows into the same room. Inside the room it is all one light."[11]

I still ask, *Can I really let God be a mystery to me? Can I let others be a mystery to me? Can I be a mystery to myself?* We feel scared of the unknown, yet I know that when I allow myself to enter love as a seeker, an explorer open to love's mysteries, I discover and rediscover love's mysterious yet revelatory ways. It's a choice *and* a grace I can pray for. I can let the mystery overtake me—its darkness and its light; its infinite possibilities; the simple and the complex; the kiss;

---

[11] Beatrice Bruteau, "Prayer and Identity," *Contemplative Review* (1983): 109.

the cup of tea; the midnight sky sparkling with stars; the deep, dark ocean. Sometimes I'm afraid to love this much.

A few years before my father passed away, I was standing in the hallway of his Palm Springs house saying goodnight. He let go of the handles of his metal walker and gave my husband a hug goodnight, then turned to me. With his hand shaking from Parkinson's, he pressed his thumb across my forehead and blessed me with the sign of the cross, something he'd been doing since I was a child. "In the name of the Father, the Son, and the Holy Spirit." I closed my eyes, and feeling his trembling hand, the basin of my heart overflowed with love.

I could feel myself forgiving the multitudes of messiness from my childhood, the decisions my father had made to further his career, resulting in our family moving half a dozen times and the constant demand on me to adjust to new schools, friends, and neighborhoods, never feeling like I belonged. There it all was—his absence, limitations, disinterest. With each stroke of my father's thumb pressing against my forehead, I could hear the echo of the words he'd by then said to me many times, "I'm sorry. I had my priorities all screwed up."

My heart wild, absorbed in God's love, was leading the way. Receiving this love pouring into us in that moment was a way my father and I were forgiving the past together. I could love this much, and more. I was not drowning. Something fierce in me held onto the primacy of love. "God is an endless ocean of love, a community of lovers united to one another in a perfect union of love," writes the theologian Ilia Delio.[12] I was discovering love with each touch—wide, expansive, and flowing like the curls of the ocean's waves. I knew I could trust it.

FROM MY SPIRITUAL JOURNAL

> *Love is seeking me. Let me be the container of your love. I see the graceful blue heron in the quiet lagoon watching intently for fish. My strong brown eyes rise with anticipation. Dear God, show me the way. Help me see what is truly before me, the visible and the invisible.*

PRAYERS AND PRACTICES

1. Remember a time when you discovered something you didn't expect—something that felt mysterious—perhaps that you liked to sing, or enjoyed spending time alone, or that the mountains were God's body.
2. Close your eyes. Let the experience come alive again. Feel it in your body and in your heart.
3. In your journal, reflect on this journey of discovering something new. Where was the Holy in this experience for you?

---

[12] Ilia Delio, *Claire of Assisi: A Heart Full of Love* (Cincinnati: Franciscan Media, 1989), 5.

3. Trusting the Mystery and Stepping Into the Unknown

A few years ago, I spent a week on the Big Island of Hawaii, housesitting for a friend. One day, my husband and I were snorkeling around an incredible coral reef at a local beach called Two Step, where we swam with large sea turtles, colorful tropical fish, and elegant angelfish. As we moved slowly through the water and away from the reef, we noticed the water below and beyond us was a deep crystal blue. As I looked at the shafts of light penetrating the water, all I could see was the vast and infinite blueness of the ocean water.

My husband and I popped our heads out of the water, took off our snorkels, and almost simultaneously exclaimed, "Whoa! This is intense." I wanted to return to shore yet was drawn to the depth and immensity of the ocean. In that moment, I met the place where I set up boundaries. *This is God*, my inner voice told me. Could I allow the Divine to become even bigger? My husband encouraged us to keep going, and as we swam further into the deep blue water, I allowed myself to expand into the mystery. I was in the temple of God, and creation was calling me to loosen my borders. I prayed to quiet the fear and allow myself to stay present with the experience of awe.

At the very moment we're breaking open and trusting more in life's mysteries, fear shows up. It's precisely at times like this that we can remember, "I am the Lord, your God, who takes hold of your right hand and says to you, Do not fear; I will help you."[13]

We live in a mystery we can never apprehend. This unknowing becomes a threshold, as we claim a sense of belonging. We are part of creation's magnitude, a part of the whole, part of the deep life of God that is our being, and we are living in. We feel the longing to become more present to this abiding mystery, to feel our connection, our belonging. We mingle with the unknown, alive in the unnamable—a beacon, a vapor, a strip of gauze. We leap toward the light of a giant star; we float on the ocean's surface; we seek and seek until we come to understand the wealth prayer offers us, how surrendering to the unknown allows our hearts to soar. God's love becomes a cradle to hold us.

* * *

On the morning of my mother's memorial Mass, I went for a swim in the Olympic-sized outdoor pool at the local recreational center. My parents' house was for sale, and I knew it would be my last visit to Palm Springs, California, and the last time I'd swim there. As I swam through the watery memories of time—I'd been visiting my parents there for thirty years—I felt life wash over me. I couldn't grasp it in my hands or hold onto it.

I was touching the intersection of life, death, and love, and I remembered that James Finley had said *all love exists in Infinite love* and trusting this love is our faith. My life,

---

[13] Isaiah 41:13-14 (NIV).

I reflected, flows from a hidden, infinite source that transcends me, yet I can feel it in the depth of my heart. As I continued swimming, I looked up at the wispy white clouds streaking across the morning sky, and with each backstroke and each breath, I felt my mother's spirit filling the heavens. Her love was now in me and beyond me and surrounding me. An absolute mystery. My heart was bursting with its awakening. Surely, Divine love was blessing me.

Love has a forever quality. We're born into Infinite love, yet we act as though it's limited, a commodity we have to find or earn or try to obtain. Within each of us, love is fulfilling itself, if we only allow ourselves to fall more deeply into its mystery. How do we get to know God in this forever way? It can happen by letting God be less defined. It can happen by letting love become so big that we are simply *in it*, not containing or controlling it. It can happen by not having to define ourselves, or others, all the time.

Mysteries need space. We need to stay close to the One who is loving us into being at every moment, the One who knows and will show us the way. The Source. The Mystery. The Indwelling Spirit. My life and God's life are one life. We need to say yes to what we don't know and cannot name. We need to stay close to the secret in our heart and, together with God, live the revelation. This can become a daily intention and a spiritual practice.

Living in the mystery takes faith. We become soul mates with God, trusting that, "We can do nothing without him, because we are never separate from him," as St. Teresa of

Avila states so clearly.[14] We awaken to the realization that there is no separation between us and God. We're in new territory. Our heart has endless layers of petals, and they all keep opening as though blossoming could go on forever.

FROM MY SPIRITUAL JOURNAL

Every day, I'm learning how to live my life, how to be in this School of Love. I'm absorbed in and constantly discovering this moist love that has birthed me from eternity. The echoes of heaven rise like a chorus, sweetly crying out to let love have a looseness. I can't fully grasp what I'm saying, but I know that doesn't matter. It's staying in the relationship of love and letting myself live in the mystery that really matter.

PRAYERS AND PRACTICES

1. Pray with the question: How am I being invited to let God be more of a mystery?

2. In your journal, reflect on the way that embracing mystery opens you up to experience more love. Use the prompt: The mystery of love makes me feel_____.

3. If your heart were singing with a chorus of angels, what would your song sound like? In this moment, overcome fear and just sing out loud to yourself the way children do, even make up a song!

---

[14] Teresa of Avila, *Interior Castle*, 48.

CLOSING REFLECTIONS

Each of us is a manifestation of love, living in communion with the Divine mystery of life and love, which is inherently trustworthy and yet feels at times to be obscure. There is an unknowing and a darkness we are asked to encounter in order to be in this becoming with God. We breathe into the softness that blurs the edge. What is outer has the dimensions of what is inner, and what is inner reaches out into all that surrounds it—atoms and skin, touching and blending.

Some days the sky is gray and heavy, birds absent, rain a possibility. On such days, deep silence slips into us, and we become a thin, fading line of doubt, uncertainty, even fear. It's easy to forget that we were born into eternal love that is always touching us, even in the smallest details and moments of our lives. Then suddenly, the heart remembers. How I love you, God, for you give me the Spirit that helps me love all things. My prayer is to let my heart grow, soar, and not be afraid how high the swing of love will carry me.

We're invited to feel this Divine touch in which the boundaries of myself and God thin and melt. Such is the Mystery acting within us. "We are born in union with God and *we live and move and have our being in God* (Acts 17:28) throughout our lives," wrote American theologian Gerald May, stating, "In keeping with the root meaning of *nature* (Natura, birth), this union with the Divine is our human nature. This is not something a person *has*, but who a person most deeply *is*: the essential spiritual nature of a human being."[15]

We can't grasp the vastness, but in the intimacy of our hearts, we sense a Presence connecting us to a wholeness—to Mystery, to Divine love, to the dark matter of the universe. We are bangles and bracelets around the Holy, and this dynamic flow of love is happening both around and within us in each act of love toward all sentient beings.

I remember the people and things I hold close. For instance, I remember once walking through the Hyatt Hotel in Palm Springs, air conditioners whirring, and the desert heat outside 110°F. My mother and I were taking our daily walk after having had a slow morning sitting with my father at the kitchen table, having a bite and sipping coffee. My father, who was suffering his final phase of Parkinson's, couldn't do much, but he loved to talk, so we sat for hours discussing anything—relationships, God, movies, work.

Each day before lunch, my father rested, so my mother and I would go out. In the heat of summer, we chose the largest hotel for a long walk. As we entered the thick glass doors, the doorman and concierge gave my mother a familiar, friendly nod.

There wasn't much to say, my mother and I were simply in that moment together. As we walked, we each took out our rosaries. Mine had wooden beads, a present my

---

[15] Gerald. G. May, *The Dark Night of the Soul: A Psychiatrist Explores the Connection Between Darkness and Spiritual Growth* (San Francisco: HarperSanFrancisco, 2005), 42-43.

parents brought back from Assisi, and my mother held slim black beads they'd gotten in Spain. The Catholic rosary is structured around four sets of mysteries: joyful, glorious, sorrowful, and luminous. That day we recited the glorious mysteries. My mother knew each one: the Resurrection, the Ascension, the Descent of the Holy Spirit, the Assumption, and the Crowning of Mary.

We both felt that saying the rosary was somehow helping my father, and we were comforted by that. The rosary connected my parents and me to God and each other throughout our lives—the pink plastic rosary I held at my first communion and prayed with on Sunday nights, the white rosary beads my mother kept under her pillow to pray with when she was awake at night, and the soft wooden beads my father held at my sister's funeral.

Walking and reciting the rosary is something I still do. Ambling through the park on the way home from work, wanting to forget the stress of the day, I pull out the same wooden rosary I've had for years, which I always keep in my purse. I hold this string of memories as mysteries of love tied to my heart and walk along with the voices of prayer held deep within me.

What is there after all this stripping away? We sit in silence, deeply dwelling in the question, only to hear ourselves say, *I don't know, but God knows.*

FURTHER JOURNAL EXPLORATION

Let us pray with poetry from *Rilke's Book of Hours: Love Poems to God* and engage in journaling to guide us into the depths of love we share mysteriously with God. Begin by slowly reading the following words from Rilke's poem, "The Book of Monastic Life, I, 2."[16]

- "I live my life in widening circles
  that reach out across the world.
  I may not complete this last one
  but I give myself to it.
  I circle around God, around the primordial tower.
  I've been circling for thousands of years
  and I still don't know: am I a falcon,
  a storm, or a great song?"
- In what way do you feel you are being invited to live your life "in widening circles" and live more in the mystery at this time in your life? Reflect on this question in your journal.
- What is a symbol of the Mystery for you? Draw a picture of it or find an image that represents it for you. Add it to your journal.

---

[16] *Rilke's Book of Hours*, 45.

THE SEVENTH INVITATION: GRATITUDE
RELAXING AND ENJOYING THE RELATIONSHIP

"Fall onto your knees in gratitude, a blessed gratitude for life."
— ST. JOHN OF THE CROSS[1]

Gratitude is a deep well within from which we can always draw. It creates the conditions for love to manifest. The word *gratitude* comes from the Latin *grata* or *gratia*—gift—and from this same root we have the word *grace*, a spontaneous, unexpected gift from God, a show of mercy regardless of merit. Gratitude as gift and gratitude as God's grace anchor us in the Sacred. Gratitude calls on us to recognize life as a gift.

Responding with gratitude to life's peaks and valleys requires presence and intention. Often we encounter resistance—ingratitude coming from anger, disappointment,

---

[1] Ladinsky, *Love Poems*, 320.

and not accepting what is. At such moments, gratefulness is a choice we can nurture and strengthen with commitment and practice.

A few years ago, I was slipping into despair. I'd been sleeping poorly for months and was going to work feeling frustrated. I was tired of being a school librarian but couldn't imagine making a change for economic reasons. It felt nearly impossible to accept my day-to-day life until I came across Angeles Arrien's book *Living in Gratitude*. Reading the introduction, I was immediately struck by her statement, "We can choose to be grateful, or we can choose to be ungrateful—to take our gifts and blessings for granted."[2]

I leaped into daily gratitude practice the way I do with swimming, plunging into the water without a moment's hesitation. Spirit was urging me, and I responded. I started and ended every day with prayers of thanks and began keeping a gratefulness journal. I said *thank you* more throughout the day, and over time I found other gratitude practices. This awakening of gratitude gave rise to more acceptance, appreciation, and contentment.

To my surprise, the effects were immediate. My food got tastier. I could see the blueness of the sky and hear the laughter of the children I read to in the library. I could relax into the comfort and warmth of my bed at night. I came face to face with how often I compared myself and at the

---

[2] Angeles Arrien, *Living in Gratitude: A Journey That Will Change Your Life* (Boulder, CO: Sounds True, 2011), 3.

same time, when I was criticizing myself. I felt the storms in my heart and observed when my mind got stuck in loops.

I accepted it all and was grateful for my willingness to do so, to encounter and accept my fatigue, frustrations, and sense of financial pressures. I was grateful for allowing my truth without running away. The more I met ingratitude with openness, the stronger the energy of gratefulness was in me. Gratitude became a kind of hospitality toward myself.

I realized I'd been carrying expectations of what gratitude looks, feels, and sounds like, and often relating to it in a dualistic way—I'm either grateful or I'm not. Slowly I began to recognize that we can be grateful *and* have a wide range of feelings and responses.

I also began to see that experiencing and expressing gratitude can happen in a variety of ways. Gratitude doesn't always look and sound the same. Going to yoga class can be an expression of gratitude for my body. Noticing the sparrows in my backyard can be an experience of gratitude for nature. Remembering someone I love who has passed away can be an expression of gratitude for the love we shared.

I began to ask myself, *What would it be like to embrace a more inclusive and expansive sense of gratitude?* Gratefulness isn't something we need to add to our lives, rather something inherent and already present. We only need to notice it from the depth of our being.

As I continued this practice, I came to the realization that our deepest transformations come not from living *with* gratitude, but from living *in* gratitude. When we live *in* something, we allow ourselves to become the thing itself. I *became* gratitude! It was not something added to my life, but a way to *be*. The title of the book *Living in Gratitude* helped me see this.

Gratitude has many dimensions. It's unlimited, forever opening in our hearts. How can it be our stance and the essence of our relationship with the Divine, others, and all of life? We can encourage gratefulness by following three guiding principles. Gratefulness needs a foundation of rest, finds expression in thankfulness, and invites us to relax and enjoy Divine presence.

1. Gratefulness arises from within and needs a foundation of rest.

"Gratefulness is the inner gesture of *giving* meaning to our life by *receiving* life as a gift," writes Brother David Steindl-Rast in his classic book, *Gratefulness, the Heart of Prayer: An Approach to Life in Fullness*. He adds, "The deepest meaning of any given moment lies in the fact that it is given. Gratefulness recognizes, acknowledges, and celebrates this meaning."[3] It's in our quiet moments—in prayer, rest, and stillness—that we can notice the awakening of a grateful spirit within, a spirit that recognizes life as a gift, a gift of each moment. Rest is integral and can take many forms. It can be a momentary pause, like saying a prayer or breathing

---

[3] David Steindl-Rast, *Gratefulness, the Heart of Prayer: An Approach to Life in Fullness* (Mahwah, NJ: Paulist Press, 1984), 207.

mindfully before a meal. It can be a time set aside for contemplation, during which we experience ourselves resting in God and God resting in us. It can be a comforting nap or a leisurely afternoon sitting in the garden. It can be a moment of silence, alone or shared.

In the busyness of our lives, we usually focus on what we want and what we need to get done, and we quickly feel ungrateful when things don't go according to plan. But when we stop and invite quietness to settle into us, we give ourselves a chance to notice what we're grateful for—the people in our lives, the smell of lavender, the contours of mountains, the generosity of love all around us. When we rest, even momentarily, we grant ourselves the time and space for reflection. This is the fertile ground from which gratitude arises naturally and allows us to make the conscious choice to turn our heart and mind toward gratefulness. We hear the opening lines from the poem, "I Go Among Trees," by Wendell Berry: "I go among trees and sit still. All my stirring becomes quiet around me like circles on water."[4]

In the book of *Genesis*, after God finishes the work of creation, God rests. We know that many animals hibernate, and deciduous plants store energy in the still, dark, and hidden places. We rest not only to restore our energy, but also to open the way for stillness. Rest allows something new to emerge. Jesus's life was one of action and rest, a rhythm of

---

[4] Wendell Berry, *This Day: Collected & New Sabbath Poems* (Berkeley, CA: Counterpoint, 2014), 7.

immersion—pouring out love, compassion, and mercy into the world—and one of withdrawal from the crowds and time alone in prayer. It wasn't rest *or* action; it was both. And he called his Apostles to rest also. "Come with me by yourselves to a quiet place and get some rest,"[5] he tells them after an extensive period of traveling and teaching.

Rest and silence are gifts we can give to ourselves and each other. There are times my husband and I like to take time out from the constant buzz of city life and spend a day in nearby Muir Woods. As we drive to the park, we don't even play music; we just allow a deep sense of silence to fill the car, and we enjoy it together. I used to be anxious, always needing to talk to feel connected. Now I realize that silence is something to enjoy and share with others. While we're there, we walk quietly through the Redwood groves and among the giant trees. "All creation holds its breath, listening within me, because to hear you, I keep silent," wrote the poet Rainer Maria Rilke.[6]

The continual practice of letting go—of the tension in the body and the chatter in the mind—helps us cultivate an inner state of restfulness. As an inner spaciousness becomes available to us, we can find silence more intentional. Cultivating more silence into our lives, we nurture restfulness and make room for gratefulness to arise naturally.

The invitation to rest challenges us to stop striving and

[5] Mark 6:30 (NIV).
[6] *Rilke's Book of Hours*, 79.

surrender into a more restful place within. When we give ourselves permission to rest, we enter into the womb of God and float in the depth of our being. It's here—alone with God—that we meet more of ourselves, not less. "Rest, my dears, in prayer," wrote St. Catherine of Siena.[7]

Prayer and contemplation help us find a sacred place within that offers rest. In prayer, we connect more consciously with the Holy, centering our hearts on God's presence. Our prayer becomes a time to enjoy divine presence, without an agenda or expectations. Sometimes, the simple act of focusing on our breath, lighting a candle, or listening to the sound of a bell allows us to find rest. As we learn to rest in the Divine, we discover that there, in the stillness, in the breath, we find God resting in us, and we are grateful.

FROM MY SPIRITUAL JOURNAL

I pause. I pray, "Be Still and Know that I am God."[8] I enter Divine shelter: a cave within a cave, a light within a light. And, I rest inside this heart of love. Morning, noon, and night, I live with the seasons of my life. For when I squeeze my life through an hourglass, I cannot remember that we are stars filling the night sky, held in place by pure grace.

---

[7] Ladinsky, *Love Poems*, 195.
[8] Psalms 46:10 (NRSV).

PRAYERS AND PRACTICES

1. Find rest in this moment by gently stopping and taking three conscious breaths. Let your breathing be easy and flow naturally.
2. Pray with the words from Psalms 62:5 (NRSV), "Yes, my soul, find rest in God." Repeat the phrase several times, letting it sink in and rest in you.
3. Write in your journal, using the following prompts: *I can find more rest for my body by____; I can find more rest for my mind by____.*

2. Gratefulness finds expression in thankfulness, in our actions and interactions.

Gratitude is a response to God's generosity. James Finley writes, "Our very being and the very being of everyone and everything around us is the generosity of God. God is creating us in the present moment, loving us into being, such that our very presence is the manifested presence of God's love."[9] And for this, our heartfelt response is thankfulness.

Divine love is continuously pouring into us, creating us into being every moment, and this awareness brings us to pray, "Let everything that breathes praise the Lord" (Psalms 150, NRSV). Seeing our lives united with Spirit allows the generosity of love to fill us. It informs our perspective, the

---

[9] James Finley, *Christian Meditation: Experiencing the Presence of God* (San Francisco: HarperSanFrancisco, 2004), 42-43.

way we feel about and see ourselves, our lives, and the world. We come to see life as a gift, and our response is thankfulness and humility.

Many of us struggle with both seeing and relating to our lives as a gift. Brother David Steindl-Rast poses the question: *Why is it so difficult to acknowledge a gift as a gift?* He believes that admitting something as a gift is also admitting our dependence on the giver. And we don't like or want to be dependent on anyone or anything. Seeing ourselves as completely independent, however, is an illusion; we are all living interdependent lives. Brother David adds, "Gratefulness always goes beyond myself. For what makes something a gift is precisely that it is given. And the receiver depends on the giver. This is true humility."[10]

Angeles Arrien writes, "Humility is a blessing, as it allows us to reach beyond ourselves and appreciate the gifts others bring to the world, a natural source of gratitude."[11] Gratitude grows in us in silence, during moments of rest. And it is nurtured when we express it aloud—to God, others, and even ourselves. Speaking something brings it to life. I might say thank you to my husband for cooking dinner, to a friend for helping me sort through a problem, to myself for taking time to go to yoga and care for my body, to Creation for the beauty of a ruby-throated hummingbird, to God for bringing me to a new day of life. The practice of saying

---

[10] Steindl-Rast, *Gratefulness, the Heart of Prayer*, 15.
[11] Arrien, *Living in Gratitude*, 153.

thank you genuinely throughout the day encourages hospitality within and around us and cultivates grateful living.

A few years ago, a friend was struggling with a recent change in her work. During one conversation over lunch, she leaned on the table and said in a clear, calm voice, "As soon as I turn on the switch of gratitude, things begin to change—maybe not outside, but inside, and that makes all the difference." Gratitude is a disposition of the heart.

Gratitude offers us an alternative way of being. It's rich and noble—filled with appreciation, contentment, blessing, praise, restfulness, thankfulness, and so much more. Gratitude begets more gratitude; it's a gift that keeps on giving. The more I say thank you—to a colleague who offers an encouraging word, to my sister for receiving my tears, and to God for this given moment—a softness descends over me like a warm blanket. "While gratitude is both a feeling and an attitude, thankfulness is the demonstrative expression of it, whether extended to ourselves or others," writes Angeles Arrien.[12]

We can find simple ways to express gratitude throughout the day: when we wake up, before we eat, after we engage in a physical activity, before we go to sleep. After I go swimming, I always pause in the locker room and say within myself, *Dear God, thank you for the time, health, and motivation to swim.* I find unity in such small gestures. I'm always with God; God is always with me. As we learn to dwell in gratitude, we shift

---

[12] Arrien, *Living in Gratitude*, 5.

our awareness to one of grateful seeing, which nurtures us in the depth of our being.

To deepen our capacity for living gratefully, we need to expand our sense of ourselves, our lives, and the Sacred. When my father was in his seventies and suffering from regret, he told me his constant prayer was, "Lord, make me grateful for all the events in my life." Gratefulness is a force, a spirit that gives us life!

There are times we can't connect to gratitude. We meet places of resistance, places where we feel stuck. In those moments, we can let ourselves *feel* the resistance, engage with interest, curiosity, and compassion, and attempt to befriend our resistance and learn from it. *What is its message?* It could be helping us see how we lose our connection to ourselves through comparison, disappointment, frustration, lack of forgiveness, or lack of self-acceptance. We realize our inability to feel gratitude is not negative. It's something deep and tender within us calling for our attention. This tension of opposites we experience can lead to transformation, especially when we respond with self-care and self-compassion.

As we begin to notice our habitual patterns, welcoming all our feelings and the thoughts that arise and addressing them as needed, we begin to cultivate an inclusive relationship with gratitude. Gratitude is a practice, and it is a healthy and valuable antidote for taking things for granted, and not recognizing life's miracles.

Another way to show agency and not be pulled down by

the lack of gratitude is exercising choice. Sometimes I physically turn my body in another direction and tell myself, "We're going this way!" This action is both symbolic and energetic. Gratitude needs our loving support and encouragement. It needs room to grow in our lives. I've found this simple teaching from Cynthia Bourgeault to be very helpful: "What you don't grab hold of, can't grab hold of you."

Gratitude is a commitment, and commitment requires recommitment, something one learns over the years in a long marriage. Heartfelt theologian and author Henri Nouwen wrote, "In the past I always thought of gratitude as a spontaneous response to the awareness of gifts received, but now I realize that gratitude can also be lived as a discipline. The discipline of gratitude is the explicit effort to acknowledge that all I am and have is given to me as a gift of love, a gift to be celebrated with joy."[13]

The more we can welcome all of ourselves, and others, and receive life as it is, the more that gratitude can transform us. We need our gratitude practice to become more honest, more sincere, and thus more trustworthy. The Divine meets us right here in the truth of our lives. Together with God, we can gaze at our lives with tenderness, compassion, grace, and gratitude.

---

[13] Henri J. M. Nouwen, *The Return of the Prodigal Son: A Story of Homecoming* (New York: Image Books, 1994), 85.

FROM MY SPIRITUAL JOURNAL

Looking for the bounty and good in my life. The blessings in disguise. I seek to see my life through the lens of love, and through a grateful heart. I long to lose myself in the abundance of the cherry blossoms—pink and white petals, delicately falling from their branches as light as snowflakes. Thank you, I whisper to the tiny petals kissing the earth.

PRAYERS AND PRACTICES

1. In the quiet of your heart, hear God saying, "Thank you," for all you are and all you do. How does it feel to share this moment with God?

2. In your journal, write using the prompt: *I can be grateful for_____, and I can feel_____.* Continue to write about any thoughts, feelings and experiences this evokes for you.

3. Gratitude is an energy. Repeat "thank you" aloud ten times the next time you feel disconnected from gratitude.

3. Relaxing and enjoying our relationship with God

On Saturday afternoons after the house is cleaned, the errands completed and the groceries put away, my husband and I have a few unstructured hours. If the sun is shining, we sit on the deck at the back of the house, put out some snacks, turn on the music, and let time spread out. We relax by freeing ourselves from the pressure of time and enjoy each other's company. When we're relaxed and taking in each other and what's around us, we experience gratefulness.

I know myself through knowing him, just as I know myself through knowing God. This is a knowing of the heart. We share a togetherness; a sacred union; a rhythm, movement, and flow from self to other to a togetherness that completes each of us. "When we reach our innermost heart," Brother David writes, "we reach a realm where we are not only intimately at home with ourselves, but intimately united with others, all others."[14]

On one of my last visits to see my ninety-one-year-old mother, she gazed at me quietly across the dining room table, and I met her soft brown eyes in silence. After a few minutes, she remarked, "It's nice just to be together and simply appreciate each other." These wise and endearing words have stayed with me and continue to inform all my relationships—with others and with the Divine. When we're aware of sacred presence, we feel a deep and abiding gratefulness.

When we're relaxed, we're more present for ourselves and those around us. Our listening becomes crisp, our eyes clear, and our hearts wide open. This is true of our relationship with God, too. The more peaceful and present we are, the more available we are to enjoy the gift of Divine love pouring into and through us, and we are grateful.

Thich Nhat Hanh teaches that to enjoy a sunset is effortless. We are born with the capacity to enjoy the gifts of

---

[14] Steindl-Rast, *Gratefulness, the Heart of Prayer*, 29.

life—the sunset, a smile, a fragrant rose. One of his mantras is: "Take my hand. We will walk. We will only walk. We will enjoy our walk without thinking of arriving anywhere."[15]

We pray to be grounded in gratitude. We continue to discover ways to relax and enjoy our relationship with God, ourselves, and each other. Sometimes it happens in the most unexpected way. On my husband's birthday a few years ago, I bought him a copy of *The Art of Simple Food* by Alice Waters. He wanted to learn to cook more, and this book with the word *simple* in the title seemed perfect. He tried a few recipes and fell in love with cooking. He started watching prominent chefs on YouTube and found cooking to be relaxing and deeply satisfying. Our partnership in the kitchen expanded, as did our connection with food and cooking.

Planning, buying, and preparing food together is an emblem of caring for each other and ourselves. It wasn't something we were just doing for ourselves, but something we were doing for each other. It was a way of feeding our union, our togetherness. It formed a foundation in our home. On weekends, we enjoy going to the farmers' market, getting fresh fruits and vegetables in season. This tending of our food together continues to be an act of love, a way of enjoying our relationship and the gift of togetherness.

We can always discover gratitude as the heart of all our relationships if we're willing to constantly meet the now. The present moment is offering us the opportunity to

---

[15] Thich Nhat Hanh, *Call Me by My True Names: The Collected Poems of Thich Nhat Hanh* (Berkeley, CA: Parallax Press, 2001).

recommit to gratitude and to renew our love. We learn that when we're grateful, we recognize and enjoy the love of God in everything.

PRAYERS AND PRACTICES

1. For three breaths, say the words "thank you" silently, and feel yourself being filled with the Spirit of gratitude.
2. Pray with the question: How can I cultivate gratitude as a habit of my heart?
3. Create an evening prayer of gratitude, which could be as simple as reminding yourself of five things you were grateful for from your day, before you fall asleep.

FROM MY SPIRITUAL JOURNAL

Everything is connected. If I've had a restless night, if my husband has had a restless night, the next day I always change the sheets. Beginning anew. Clean sheets. Changing the sheets on the bed is an act of love. I feel the melting of tenderness in my bones as I bend to curl them around the mattress and tuck in the blankets. Every night, I pray in the dark gratitude for this love.

CLOSING REFLECTIONS

Gratitude is a grace that allows us to find acceptance in difficult situations. Brother David Steindl-Rast teaches that it's possible to be grateful simply for the opportunity to be grateful, that the gifts of gratitude are healing and allow us to be more compassionate, forgiving, and accepting of ourselves and others. Love is always something to be thankful for; through love relationships, we're always being stretched. The gift in any situation is the possibility to learn, to grow, to enjoy, to struggle, and to love more. "Gratefulness is the gallantry of a heart ready to rise to the opportunity a given moment offers," writes Brother David.[16]

As I was preparing the eulogy for my mother's memorial Mass, the notion of gratitude became my starting point. Although my relationship with my mother had been both joyous and sorrowful, through the window of gratitude I could see her life as a gift to my large family—the gift of her love, her faith, and all we shared together. Even the difficult times were gifts, teaching me to grow in love beyond what I thought possible.

Love is trustworthy, even though human relationships can be fragile at times. Because we love, we will experience great pain and loss, as well as great fulfillment. She was my mother. I was her eighth child. She loved me; she hurt me. She held me; she neglected me. I loved her; I hurt her. I held her; I rejected her. We journeyed far together.

As I grew older and understood my mother's life better, her longings and disappointments, I developed compassion for her. When I was six, my mother wanted to attend college, so she left my two younger sisters and me at home with a

---

[16] Steindl-Rast, *Gratefulness, the Heart of Prayer*, 210.

nanny and housekeeper while she learned sociology, art history, and English literature. She craved knowledge and imagined a formal education would make her feel more confident next to my father, a neurosurgeon. But after graduation, she crashed. All that knowledge hadn't changed her in the ways she'd hoped and expected. She sank into despair and entered seven years of alcoholism. It was devastating for all of us: her absence, her indulgence, her neglect. As a child, I was always missing my mother and wanting more of her.

Then as an adult, I found that my mother understood me as I faced my own dark night of the soul, with infertility, insomnia, financial strains, and the ups and downs of marriage. She *knew* heartbreak, struggle, and disappointment. She truly had a compassionate heart, and became a source of comfort for me, listening to my deep despair and receiving my endless tears with a mother's tenderness. With her, I could be honest and didn't need to hide in shame for things not working out. She was willing to sit with me in the darkness. She was now a recovered alcoholic, and through her years of suffering, she grew in love, in her relationship with God, and in her faith.

She taught me to have faith, too, as I began to discover the Divine love relationship stirring so deeply within, as I touched a longing for the Divine heart beating in mine. I journeyed with my mother as she lost my father, as she faced living alone as a widow, as she began to depend on a walker to get around. Through it all, through loving her, through our relationship, my heart stretched beyond what

I thought it was capable of—for that is the gift of love. If we let ourselves receive love fully, it invites us to bring the power and presence of gratitude into our hearts, and to see life through the heart of gratefulness.

FURTHER JOURNAL EXPLORATION

In this section, we pray with the writing of Brother David Steindl-Rast and engage in spiritual journaling as a way to nourish our souls and nurture a grateful heart.

- Read the following quote from David Steindl-Rast slowly, several times:

  Everything is a gift. The degree to which we are awake to this truth is a measure of our gratefulness, and gratefulness is a measure of our aliveness.

- Notice a word or phrase in this quote from Brother David that stands out for you. For a few moments, let that word or phrase dwell in your heart. Discover what this word or phrase means to you at this time in your spiritual journey.
- Write in your journal about what you discovered. And create a drawing that expresses how you feel.

PART III

LIVING LOVE

We are born into a great invitation of love.

When I began writing this book, I was focused on the call, "You shall love the Lord your God with all your heart, and with all your soul, and with all your strength, and with all your mind." As I continue to follow this path, I hear clearly the rest of the call, "... and love your neighbor as yourself."[1]

In *Teachings on Love*, Thich Nhat Hanh states clearly that the capacity to love others depends on the capacity to love ourselves,[2] not in a self-absorbed way, but with a compassionate and unified heart. We're not being called to love our neighbor "as much" as we love ourselves, but rather to love our neighbor "as" ourselves, with the awareness that

---

[1] Luke: 10:27 (NRSV)
[2] Thich Nhat Hanh, *Mindful Living: A Collection of Teachings on Love, Mindfulness, and Meditation* (Boulder, CO: Sounds True, 2001), CD.

everyone is a manifestation of Divine love.[3] Everyone and everything belongs and is loved. We are all siblings of the infinite source of love. I see the mountains as God's body and the oceans as God's generous heart.

Over and over, in my life and in writing this book, I have learned to say *yes*—yes to belonging, yes to love, yes to being an integral part of the cosmic dance. We each must take our place and say, "Yes!" We're a part of the vastness, living in intimacy with the Divine. Love is the most generous and healing energy. The more we're able to recognize ourselves as manifestations of Divine love and cultivate connections to this energy, the more we are able to see everyone and everything as expressions of the sacred and understand the connection between God, us, others, the Earth, and the cosmos.

Divine love is our common ground, and we are all invited to awaken to the presence and action of this love in our hearts and our lives. We are all embodiments of Divine love. The Oneness of this love is in our deepest being and our cells, in every stone, every star, each snowflake and heartbeat: matter and spirit dwelling in every particle of life. As we come to see this intermingling, we can live from this realization through an open, illumined heart.

By saying yes, we allow ourselves to be open and vulnerable to life, just as it is. We follow our intuition, our longing and our curiosity. We choose to stay in the flow of life and love and expand our capacity to embrace all that life presents.

---

[3] Cynthia Bourgeault, offered for the Living School Symposium, New Mexico, August 2018.

Fruits of Intimacy

In our small backyard stands a Fuji apple tree, the center-piece of our garden. Although we live in the fog belt in San Francisco, with wet and chilly summers, fruit still grows. Every year, we watch the cycle from tiny blossoms to pink apples, as we faithfully water, prune, and fertilize. My husband and I have found that by caring for our apple tree, we are reminded of the importance of tending whatever we want to grow in our lives.

Two summers ago, a pair of blue jays discovered our tree, picking their way through every piece of fruit before it ripened. On the tree hung half-eaten apples turning brown. We were heartbroken. The following year we put mesh netting around the tree, but the wind blew it askew, allowing the birds to find a way in. Once again, they picked through all the apples, and we felt crushed.

We searched for an answer to no avail. And then one day while driving through the wine country in Napa County, we noticed spiral reflectors in the vineyards. We decided to try them, placing the shiny deterrents on the outer branches of the tree. To our surprise, it worked. In late September, we didn't see any squawking jays looming around, and the apples grew plump until they were ready to harvest.

The nature of an apple tree is to produce ripe fruit, just as the nature of intimacy with the Divine is to produce bountiful love and care for the world. The fruits of intimacy with the Divine are measured in compassion and self-giving. The tree gives us apples to eat. The heart of love gives compassion and care to self, others, and the world. We tend the apple tree so it can provide fruit for all. We tend our hearts so they can become sources of generous love for all. Each one of us is connected to and living in the wholeness of love.

The journey with our apple tree reminded me how the fruit and the tree are inseparable. Our hearts and the heart of the world are also inseparable. Our inner and outer journeys are woven together. Divine love dwells deep in the sanctuary inside our hearts, *and* in the daily walk of our lives. The spiritual heart is unified, teaching us to see the whole, not just the parts. We notice how our relationship to Divine love touches and reaches deep within us *and* deep beyond us, around us, and in the world. Is our love relationship with the Divine producing more compassion for self, others, and the world around us?

Pema Chödrön states, "Compassion for others begins with kindness to ourselves." And love and compassion toward ourselves creates an opening within that calls us to care for others. The other day at school, a petite, second-grade girl was running down the hall, against the rules, and slammed right into me. "I'm sorry," she kept saying. As I looked into her anxious brown eyes, I could tell she knew her mistake, and I felt my heart open in compassion. So, rather than reprimand her, I asked, "Are you okay?" We're free to choose the path of compassion at any time—in what we say or don't say, do or don't do.

Connecting with the compassion that abides in our

hearts allows us to share that compassion—in seemingly simple situations as well as more complex circumstances. The awakening of a compassionate heart is needed to hold the brokenness of life with love and hope. Jesus's love is compassionate. In the Gospel of Mark, we hear that when Jesus saw a large crowd waiting for him at the edge of the water as he was arriving by boat, he felt compassion for them, because they were like sheep without a shepherd. So, he began teaching them.[4]

Through a steady and faithful practice of prayer, self-awareness, discernment, and loving action, we can notice the quality of our individual love relationship with the Divine and the quality of the love we share in and with the world. We're invited always to let our love reach out and touch others, to be generous. At the end of *Interior Castle*, the great mystic Teresa of Avila emerges from the depth of her inner awakening only to say, "We should desire and engage in prayer, not for our enjoyment, but for the sake of acquiring this strength which fits us for service."[5]

"... *the fruit of the Spirit is love, joy, peace, patience, kindness, generosity, faithfulness, gentleness and self-control. There is no law against such things.*"[6] These fruits all grow out of living in the flow of God's love. Father Thomas Keating wrote, "The Fruits of the Spirit are indications of God's presence at work in us in varying degrees and forms."[7] And I believe the same

---

[4] Mark 6:34 (NRSV).
[5] Teresa of Avila, *Interior Castle*, 231.
[6] Galatians 5:22-23 (NRSV).
[7] Keating, *Fruits and Gifts of the Spirit*, 13.

is true for the fruits of intimacy. As we grow in intimacy with the Divine, we are becoming love. By living the seven invitations to love that came to me that wondrous Sunday afternoon in my art studio, and which I have reflected on and explored ever since, we are joining in the generous out-pouring and indwelling of Divine love.

It is through the indwelling Spirit, acting within us, that we enter into God's love. We allow the infilling and the outpouring of love to be a constant flow in our hearts and a constant expression in our lives. God fills us; we share this love; God fills us; we share this love. Until we come to understand that we are never without it. Until we know that, in essence, we *are* this abundant love.

More and more, we stabilize ourselves in this intimate and growing love. We trust in the Presence of love, which is constant, steadfast, always here and now; even though it moves and flows like wind, water, and blood. Self-knowledge is key. In the Gospels, we often hear of Jesus healing the blind, restoring their ability to see that they are beloved sons and daughters of God. Our task is to learn and see who we really are. In her essay, "Prayer and Identity," Beatrice Bruteau challenges us to see ourselves as more than our self-descriptions, more than the narrative sense we hold of ourselves or how society identifies us. We can all too easily lose sight that our true identity is love, and a oneness with the Source of love.[8]

All aspects of life become the path, the teacher, and the

[8] Bruteau, "Prayer and Identity," 100-101.

way of practice. To stabilize ourselves in love is to seek a life of union with the Divine, with Creation, with everyone and everything, and to live in an ever growing, and ever abiding relationship to Divine love. I have heard the contemplative teacher James Finley say many times in his various talks, "Love alone has the power to name who we are and what we are."

Hearing the Invitation

The sound of church bells has been calling me since I was a child: into the Catholic church for Mass, the house of God that resides in my soul, and my inner sanctuary where I can dwell quietly. Something in me pauses at the sound of a sacred bell—it's a reminder, an invitation, a call. At home, I like to use a meditation bell, and at work I have a hand-sized brass bell that I ring to call my students to attention or to begin a moment of silence.

I've always been drawn to church bells. Their ancient sound resonates deep within me. Their ringing penetrates the air and settles in my heart. My entire being is held, and I hear the bell as a call to listen, return inside, and awaken. These rhythmic and reverberating sounds are holy and have called me many times into a holy encounter.

In the last decade, I have made two retreats to the Abbey of Gethsemane, in Kentucky, and both times I noticed how the constant tolling of the heavy, iron-cast bells creates an outer rhythm to my days and nights, and an inner rhythm to my soul. I immediately abandon myself to the sound of these bells, following the daily routine of the Cistercian monks, who are called to prayer seven times a day. The bells wake me for 3:15 a.m. vigils and invite me into the great silence after the 7:30 p.m. Compline.

Years ago, as I walked through the large wooden doors of St. Ignatius Church in San Francisco on Holy Thursday, I heard the bells permeating the night air, the depth of their clanging sound carrying me into sacred space and time. There I was again, responding to the invitation of the bells, ringing, chiming, tolling, reverberating, always inviting me home, inviting me to come inside, to greater intimacy.

Bells have always been inviting me into a relationship with God, and their sacred sound awakens and deepens this loving relationship. I have been hearing these bells ringing all of my life through passages and obstacles, sorrows and joys, in times of emptiness and fullness. The bells repeatedly invite me into an intimate love relationship with God, no matter what else is happening in my life.

I invite you to hear each of these seven invitations as a bell, calling you to your intimate love relationship with the Divine, yourself, others, and creation. Let your heart awaken to the inner and outer landscape of love in which you are already living, until love transforms you into itself and blossoms like a rose with all its beauty and fullness.

Acknowledgments

This book has been a journey of faith. Although it began as a graced moment of inspiration, the completed book is a result of the support, encouragement, and guidance of many special people. First, I want to thank my husband, Mark, who has such faith in me and believes in my path of deepening my experience of love in all its manifestations. I also would like to thank the members of the community of the Living School for Action and Contemplation for their commitment to broadening and deepening the notions of Christian love. In particular, I wish to thank James Finley, Richard Rohr, and Cynthia Bourgeault for their wisdom, teaching, and mentorship. Without them, I doubt I could have brought this book to fruition. I greatly thank Arnie Kotler, developmental editor extraordinaire, who helped me discover the depth of this book, and for his commitment to this project. I extend a heartfelt thanks to Leslie Kirk Campbell, teacher, writer, and friend, who encouraged me to stay true to my voice and helped shape the early drafts of the book. I warmly thank Julie Isaac for her coaching and companionship while working on this book. I wish to thank my spiritual director, Janice Farrell, in whose presence I touched the depth of my passion for the Divine Heart. I also would like to express deep gratitude to my friends, spiritual companions, and my loving sisters, Madeleine, Monique, Claire, and Marie, for all their support and love. Finally, a heartfelt thanks to publisher Paul Cohen, editor Susan Piperato, and the entire team at Monkfish Book Publishing Company for believing in this project and bringing it out into the world.

COLETTE LAFIA
SAN FRANCISCO
FEBRUARY 2020

ABOUT THE AUTHOR

 Colette Lafia is a San Francisco-based writer, spiritual director, speaker, and retreat leader. A graduate of the Mercy Institute for Spiritual Direction at Mercy Center in Burlingame, California, Colette recently completed the Living School program in the Christian contemplative and mystical traditions at the Center for Action and Contemplation, guided by Richard Rohr, Cynthia Bourgeault, and James Finley. Colette designs and facilitates both online and in-person retreats, and is an adjunct faculty member at Mercy Center in Burlingame. She is the author of *Comfort and Joy: Simple Ways to Care for Ourselves and Others* (Conari, 2008) and *Seeking Surrender: How My Friendship with a Trappist Monk Taught Me to Trust and Embrace Life* (Sorin Books, 2015). Colette has a passion for helping people connect more deeply with the presence of the sacred in their daily lives. Please visit her website at colettelafia.com.

CPSIA information can be obtained
at www.ICGtesting.com
Printed in the USA
JSHW022222110321
12491JS00002B/2